This b
sel

M   .in Speech and Language Pathology Series

Clinical Education in
Speech–Language Pathology

Clinical Education in Speech–Language Pathology

LINDY MCALLISTER BSPTHY, MA(HONS) (SPEECH PATH), PHD
Associate Professor, School of Community Health,
Charles Sturt University, Albury, NSW, Australia

and

MICHELLE LINCOLN BAPPSC (SPEECH PATH), PHD
Senior Lecturer and Director of Clinical Education, School of
Communication Sciences and Disorders, University of Sydney,
Sydney, NSW, Australia

Series Editors
Martin Ball, University of Louisiana at Lafayette
Alison Ferguson, University of Newcastle, New South Wales
and **Tom Powell**, University of Louisiana at Lafayette

W
WHURR PUBLISHERS
LONDON AND PHILADELPHIA

© 2004 Whurr Publishers Ltd
First published 2004
by Whurr Publishers Ltd
19b Compton Terrace
London N1 2UN England and
325 Chestnut Street, Philadelphia PA 19106 USA

Reprinted 2005

British Library Cataloguing in Publication Data

A catalogue record for this book
is available from the British Library.

ISBN 1 86156 310 8

Typeset by Adrian McLaughlin, a@microguides.net
Printed and bound in the UK by Athenæum Press Ltd, Gateshead,
Tyne & Wear.

Contents

Preface

Clinical education offers unique learning opportunities for both students and clinical educators. Students must learn from their clinical educators, although clinical educators can choose to learn from their students. If they make this choice, the ensuing learning journey is likely to be rewarding both personally and professionally. The central theme of this book is about the personal and professional growth that can be achieved by students and clinical educators learning together. We argue and illustrate how they can support and enhance each other's learning in a range of domains.

Other books on clinical education in speech–language pathology have been written for clinical educators only; this book is unique in that it is written for both students and clinical educators. It introduces a new concept of clinical educators as life-long learners as well as teachers. The book explores in detail, with practical examples and exercises, how clinical educators can learn from their students and vice versa.

This book is unique in its inclusion of the voices of clinical educators and students, describing and discussing their experiences of clinical education and interactions with each other and peers in the clinical education setting. These voices are heard in the quotes and vignettes used throughout the book. They make the theory and strategies we present come alive and aid the reader to apply these concepts to their own endeavours. These voices come from three sources. The voices of clinical educators are drawn from the doctoral thesis study of the first author Lindy McAllister. This study used narrative inquiry and phenomenology to explore with clinical educators the question 'What is it like to be a clinical educator?' The theoretical model that arose from the interview and observational data is presented in Chapter 1 and has been used in other chapters of the book. The voices of the students come from the work of one of Lindy McAllister's masters research students – Eva Nemeth – who is using phenomenology to explore with students the question 'What is it like to fail a clinical placement?' Additional student voices heard in this book come from our own experiences as clinical educators.

This book is also unique in that it honestly acknowledges the challenges and frustrations of becoming and being a clinical educator and of being a student. The emotional highs and lows and the cognitive demands are discussed. However, we hope that we have also portrayed the other side of the coin – the humour, stimulation, and deep personal and professional satisfaction possible, and the rewards that come with learning together with students. It should be noted that the book is aspirational, not prescriptive. We have avoided lists of things that should be done; instead, we have presented a vision of what students and clinical educators engaged in learning relationships might achieve.

The aims of this book are:

• To argue for a humanistic focus to clinical education which is encapsulated in the learning relationships of students and clinical educators.
• To highlight what can be learned together by students and clinical educators.
• To provoke reflection on professional practice and personal development by clinical educators and students.
• To provide a theoretical and philosophical framework for clinical education practice without dense theory.
• To provide practical principles and strategies that can be applied to everyday clinical education situations.
• To suggest a pathway of professional development from novice student to professional artistry in clinical education.
• To provide strategies for promoting professional development in clinical education, beginning in the student years and continuing into life-long speech–language pathology careers.

Although we are two Australian clinical educators, we have written a book mindful of the differences in speech–language pathology education in the English-speaking world. Professional preparation for speech–language pathologists in Australia, the United Kingdom and New Zealand have two entry points: bachelor degrees and master's degrees, whereas the USA and Canada have only master's degrees as entry points to the profession. To deal with this, we have discussed students in terms of being at novice, intermediate or entry level stages, so the information presented can be applicable to any university programme. Also, although this book is written for speech–language pathologists and students, the content is applicable to any health or education profession.

The book begins by introducing the idea that students and clinical educators can learn together. We suggest that growth and development for clinical educators and students can occur as parallel processes, each supporting the other's learning. Chapter 2 discusses how clinical educators and students can prepare for engaging in the clinical education process and Chapter 3 considers factors that contribute to the development of learning relationships in clinical education. We go on to discuss problems that may arise in learning relationships and some strategies for managing them. Chapters 4 and 5 provide an in-depth discussion of the development of personal and cognitive skills. Both chapters contain strategies, examples, learning exercises and checklists for developing skills in these areas. Chapter 6 discusses the learning processes that can be applied in clinical education and Chapter 7 moves on to discussing how learning can be assessed in clinical settings and, more importantly, how to facilitate learning through assessment. Chapter 8 then concludes the book by outlining a plan for developing skills in clinical education.

We hope that the book conveys to readers our passion for learning and our enjoyment of both the clinical education process and our students. We are aware that we are still growing and developing as people, clinicians and clinical educators, even after a combined 45 years of work as clinical educators. As current (ML) and past (LM) managers of large clinical education programmes, we have faced many challenges and we know that it is not easy to live out our core values and philosophies as discussed in this book. However, in striving to do so, we have contributed to the growth and development of our students and enriched our own work and personal lives also. We keep striving for artistry in clinical education because in doing so we continue to learn. We hope this book inspires other students and clinical educators to reaffirm the value of learning together.

Lindy McAllister and Michelle Lincoln
October 2003

To Diana Maloney, teacher, mentor, colleague and friend.
With out heartfelt thanks.

CHAPTER 1

Clinical education as professional development for both clinical educators and students

Students and clinical educators often view clinical placements as being only about students: students' development as professionals, students' learning and students being assessed. It is true that student learning outcomes and the completion of formal assessments of students' learning are tangible outcomes of placements, but, in fact, students are not the only ones growing and developing, learning and being assessed on placements. Whether we like it or not, clinical educators are being assessed too by their students (formally or informally), and clinical educators also grow and learn through the experience of having students. Clinical education offers opportunities to both educators and students for professional growth. In this chapter we suggest that growth and development for clinical educators and students can occur as parallel processes, each supporting the other's learning.

If we accept that clinical placements provide opportunities for professional development for both students and clinical educators, we need to consider the goals and stages of professional development, and models of clinical education, that support professional development for both clinical educators and students. This chapter considers these issues and subsequent chapters deal with processes in clinical education, and how these can be applied in parallel to support growth and development for both clinical educators and students.

Professional development to where?

Professional growth and development imply movement along a continuum of professional skills and competencies. Dreyfus and Dreyfus (1986) described the continuum of skill acquisition in professionals as moving from novice to expert status. This concept was used by Benner (1984) to describe the professional development of nurses, and subsequently the terms 'novice', 'advanced beginner' and 'competent practitioner' have also been used to describe student development in many clinical compe-tence assessment protocols of university students. However, there has been little work done that explores and describes the development of stu-dents and clinical educators. A discussion of the goals of clinical education may assist in clarifying what students and clinical educators can potentially achieve from their learning experiences.

Goals of clinical education

We would suggest that there are four generic goals for professional devel-opment of clinical educators and students:

1. Continuous development of clinical knowledge and skills
2. Development of knowledge and skills in education
3. Development of personal and interpersonal knowledge and skills
4. Development of cognitive skills.

These goals have subgoals that relate specifically to students and clini-cal educators. There is some overlap between subgoals, consistent with the holism of professional practice.

Generic goal 1: continuous development of clinical knowledge and skills

The subgoals for students and clinical educators of this goal of continu-ous development of clinical knowledge and skills are listed in Table 1.1.

Table 1.1 Generic goal 1: continuous development of clinical knowledge and skills

Students	Clinical educators
Preparation for complex dynamic work environments	Development of clinical expertise
Development of generic attributes	Development of professional artistry as a clinical educator
Facilitation of life-long learning	
Development of social responsibility and cross-cultural competence	
Development of clinical expertise	

Students

For students, the continuous development of clinical knowledge and skills would be directed not only towards the development of clinical competence in speech–language pathology, but also towards the development of the broad capabilities that are required for working in complex, changing environments. The goals of clinical education that relate to the continuous development of clinical knowledge and skills for students are discussed under four major areas:

1. Preparation for complex dynamic work environments
2. Development of generic attributes
3. Facilitation of life-long learning
4. Development of social responsibility and cross-cultural competence.

Other possible goals for clinical education can be found in Appendix 1.1 at the end of the chapter.

Preparation for complex dynamic work environments

There is an increasing emphasis on generic goals for clinical education to enable graduates to work successfully in complex, changing environments. Graduates of health science education programmes are expected to be competent in the practice of their discipline, i.e. to be able to apply the basic sciences and applied sciences to the care and management of clients, and to be adept and professional in their interactions with colleagues and clients. They are also expected to develop competence in what Schön (1987) describes as the 'indeterminate zones of practice' (p. 11), those grey areas of 'uncertainty, uniqueness, and value conflict [which] escape the canons of technical rationality' (p. 6), when clients' lifespans are limited and the costs of support services and intervention are high, and professionals may face ethical dilemmas when offering intervention to enhance the quality of remaining life. Clinical education that seeks to promote competence in these grey areas must use different theories of teaching and learning to those used in instruction and supervision, for competent discipline-specific practice.

Schön (1983, 1987) argued for the development of the reflective practitioner. Many clinical education programmes have a major goal to produce reflective practitioners and have constructed reflective practice (Mandy, 1989; Heinrich, 1992; Stockhausen and Creedy, 1994; Lincoln et al., 1997b). Learning processes that promote reflective practice are discussed in Chapter 6.

Development of generic attributes

In addition to being prepared to function in complex and uncertain environments, university graduates are expected to develop generic attributes that enable them to function in diverse settings and roles. These attributes include a variety of knowledge skills, thinking skills, personal skills, attributes and values, and professional and technical skills and literacies. Engel (1995) suggested that health graduates should also have broad competencies, including the ability to adapt to change and participate in change, to communicate for a range of purposes, to collaborate in groups or teams, and to be self-directed life-long learners who can apply critical reasoning and a scientific approach to decision-making in unfamiliar situations.

Facilitation of life-long learning

With the knowledge explosion occurring in all disciplines, speech–language pathology graduates are expected to be critical consumers of information and to be life-long learners who maintain competence, expand and test their own knowledge and skills, and contribute to the expansion of knowledge in the field. Professional practice in the clinical setting requires speech–language pathologists to be life-long learners. Candy et al. (1994) discussed the development of life-long learning through undergraduate education. They have profiled the qualities or characteristics of life-long learners, which are shown in Table 1.2. To be a life-long learner, it is essential to be aware of your learning style and approaches to learning, to have the ability to access learning resources, to self-direct and self-evaluate your learning, and to learn from your assessment by others. The ability to collaborate with other professionals in learning and in service delivery is also vital. Employers value such attributes and the changing nature of professional practice demands them. The clinical education setting is ideal for stimulation of the development of many of these attributes.

Development of social responsibility and cross-cultural competence

Higgs and Hunt (1999) have suggested a new goal for health science education, that of producing interactional professionals. They describe an interactional professional as a person who has technical competence as well as the attributes of interpersonal competence, the ability to interact with and change the context of practice, and the capacity to demonstrate professional responsibility in serving and enhancing society. The development of social responsibility and cross-cultural competence would be necessary to achieve the last of these attributes. Cultural diversity is a global phenomenon (Pickering and McAllister, 1997). Almost certainly, health professionals of the future will find themselves working cross-culturally, either in their own countries or internationally. Increasingly, higher education has embraced a goal of developing commitments to global responsibility and social justice in graduates (see, for example, Millwater and Yarrow, 1992) who are encouraged actively to seek out

Table 1.2 Profile of life-long learners

An inquiring mind
A love of learning
A sense of curiosity and question asking
A critical spirit
Comprehension monitoring and evaluation

Helicopter vision
A sense of the interconnectedness of fields
An awareness of how knowledge is created in at least one field of study, and an understanding of the methodological and substantive limitations of the field
Breadth of vision

Information literacy
Knowledge of major current resources available in at least one field of study
Ability to frame researchable questions in at least one field of study
Ability to locate, evaluate, manage and use information in a range of contexts
Ability to retrieve information using a variety of media
Ability to decode information in a variety of forms: written, statistical, graphs, charts, diagrams and tables
Critical evaluation of information

A sense of personal agency
A positive concept of yourself as capable and autonomous
Self-organizational skills (time management, goal-setting, etc.)

A repertoire of learning skills
Knowledge of your own strengths, weaknesses and preferred learning style
Range of strategies for learning in whatever context you find yourself
An understanding of the differences between surface and deep level learning

Adapted from Candy et al. (1994)

opportunities to create new services in areas of need in indigenous communities (Bortz et al., 1992; Jager, 1994) and communities in the developing world (Keating, 1993; Henley, 1997; Henley and Twible, 1997; McAllister and Whiteford, 2002). This trend in practice has necessitated new goals for clinical education programmes such as developing cross-cultural competence and intercultural communication skills in students (Mullavey-O'Byrne, 1999; Isaac, 2002).

Clinical educators

For clinical educators, continuous development of clinical knowledge and skills would encompass the ongoing development of clinical expertise and the development of professional artistry as a clinical educator.

Development of clinical expertise

A discussion of what constitutes clinical expertise in speech–language pathology practice is beyond the scope of this book. Unlike in nursing (see, for example, Benner, 1984), there has been little research into clinical expertise in our profession, although various speciality practice documents such as those published by the American Speech–Language–Hearing Association (1982a,b; 2000) and the description of competence in experienced speech–language pathologists in the UK (Kathleen Williamson, personal communication, 2003) suggest what expertise might look like in our profession.

Development of professional artistry

Professional artistry, as discussed by Fish and Coles (1998), takes a view of practice as complex, holistic and creative, with an interpretive attention to the details and complexities of practice. They see the professional as accountable 'for skills of course, but also for much more important moral and ethical matters that underpin their decision-making and judgement. Here to be professional is to be morally answerable for all of one's conduct, and for one's conduct as a whole, not just for parts of it' (p. 34). Frameworks and rules of thumb, rather than rules, are used. Both the means and the ends of practice are valued. Moral and professional judgement and accountability for judgements are highlighted.

We would suggest that the professional artist in clinical education has mature ethical and clinical reasoning, and is able to demonstrate and articulate this to colleagues and students. The clinical educator as professional artist would be able to recognize ethical dilemmas as they pertain to both clients and students, apply ethical reasoning to appreciate multiple perspectives on such dilemmas, and identify possible courses of action to resolve or manage such dilemmas. The clinical educator as professional artist would also use and articulate different types of clinical reasoning (Higgs and Jones, 2000), depending on the needs of clients and students, and the context in which the clinical or educational problem presents. Ethical and clinical reasoning are considered further in Chapter 5.

The professional artistry view of practice sees 'quality as coming from deepening insight into one's values, priorities, actions' (Fish and Twinn, 1997, p. 45). Research with clinical educators (McAllister, 2001) suggests that professional artistry comes with insight into our values, priorities and actions as clinical educators, and experience and commitment to growth and development. In the second section of this chapter, we present a model of the experience of being a clinical educator that emerged from McAllister's (2001) research with clinical educators. We present this as a background to a discussion of goals and stages of professional development for clinical educators.

Generic goal 2: development of knowledge and skills in education

Clearly, clinical educators need to develop skills in education in order to do their job effectively. Concepts pertinent to this goal are developed in Chapters 2, 6 and 7. Students also need to develop their skills in the education of clients, their families and other students. Competencies expected of students at the point of graduation (see, for example, Speech Pathology Association of Australia, 2001) include the ability to educate clients, families, other professionals involved with speech–language pathology clients and the wider community. An increasingly common example is that of educating new mothers' groups about normal communication and literacy development and ways to stimulate these in the home. Students are also increasingly involved in peer group learning (Ladyshewsky, 1993; Lincoln and McAllister, 1993). Sometimes these are peers at the same level of professional education; at other times they might be students in more junior years, e.g. Rosenthal (1986) described a system of pairing senior (year 4) students with novice (year 2) students just beginning clinical practice. The year 4 students were responsible for educating the year 2 students about clinic procedures and basic clinical skills teaching. Students need to have basic skills in teaching and assessment to fulfil these roles (Table 1.3).

Table 1.3 Generic goal 2: development of knowledge and skills in education

Students	Clinical educators
Gaining skills in educating clients, carers, colleagues and peers	Gaining skills and knowledge in clinical education models and techniques

Effective and satisfying interactions with clients, colleagues, educators and student peers require both clinical educators and students to have personal knowledge and skills and excellent interpersonal communication skills. Concepts pertinent to this goal are developed in Chapters 3 and 4.

Generic goal 3: development of personal and interpersonal knowledge and skills

Table 1.4 Generic goal 3: development of personal and interpersonal knowledge and skills

Students	Clinical educators
Development of professional communication skills Development of self-knowledge and self-awareness Development of time management abilities	Extension of self-knowledge and self-awareness Extending counselling skills into the area of clinical education Developing awareness of one's need for control Extension of time management abilities

Generic goal 4: development of cognitive skills

Clinical practice involves using different types of knowledge (personal, theoretical and practical) and ethical and clinical reasoning skills. Concepts pertinent to this goal are developed in Chapter 5.

Table 1.5 Generic goal 4: development of cognitive skills

Students	Clinical educators
Development of clinical reasoning skills	Ability to articulate both clinical and ethical reasoning processes
Development of ethical reasoning skills	Ability to articulate professional craft knowledge
Development of skills in reflection	Ability to identify different types of knowledge used in the clinical reasoning process

Having considered goals of professional development achievable in the context of clinical education, the next section goes on to consider the types of models that might support the attainment of the goals for clinical educators and students outlined above.

Models of clinical education

There are many models of clinical education (see McLeod et al., 1997, for a review of these), but few relate to a view of clinical education as an opportunity for professional development for both students and their clinical educators. This section discusses four models that can be applied to our discussion of clinical education as affording professional development for both students and clinical educators. The first model is that of being a clinical educator, which is grounded in research with clinical educators (McAllister, 2001). As there is no research that has examined the experience of being a speech–language pathology student, the second model is an adaptation of the first model which seeks to highlight common elements. The third and fourth models – Anderson's (1988) Continuum of Supervision and the Integrative Task–Maturity Model of Supervision by Mawdsley and Scudder (1989) – provide developmental perspectives of the clinical education processes for students and clinical educators.

Model 1: a model of the experience of being a speech–language pathology clinical educator

This model is grounded in data from a research project conducted by one of the authors, McAllister (2001). The experience of being a clinical educator was studied using phenomenology (Crotty, 1996) and narrative enquiry (Clandinin and Connelly, 1991). Analysis of the data from repeated observations and in-depth interviews with five clinical educators with a range of experience yielded six major dimensions of experience:

1. A sense of self
2. A sense of relationship with others
3. A sense of being a clinical educator
4. A sense of agency
5. Seeking dynamic self-congruence
6. Growth and development.

Each of these major dimensions, or themes, had subthemes, as shown in Table 1.6. The dimensions are discussed in detail below.

Table 1.6 Dimensions and elements of the model of the experience of being a clinical educator

Dimension 1: a sense of self	**Dimension 2: a sense of relationship with others**
Elements	Elements
Having self-awareness and self-knowledge	Being people oriented
Having self-acceptance	Perceiving others
Having a self-identity	Values in relating to others
Choosing a level of control	Seeking to implement values and
Being a life-long learner	perceptions in relating to others
Dimension 3: a sense of being a clinical educator	**Dimension 4: a sense of agency as a clinical educator**
Elements	Elements
Understanding of role	Perceptions of competence and
Motivations for becoming a clinical educator	capacity to act as a clinical educator
Desired approaches to clinical education	Creating and maintaining facilitative learning environments
Affective aspects of being a clinical educator	Designing, managing and evaluating students' learning programmes
	Managing self
	Managing others
Dimension 5: seeking dynamic self-congruence	**Dimension 6: growth and development – possible stages and pathways**
Elements	Elements
Bringing a higher level of attention to the role	Embarking on the journey of becoming a clinical educator
Drawing the selves together	Moving from novice to advanced beginner
Striving for plan–action congruence	Developing competence in the role
	Pursuing professional artistry
	Suffering burnout

From McAllister (2001)

Sense of self

The core phenomenon in this study was 'sense of self', which influenced how you related to others, approached being a clinical educator, and took action in the workplace. Although not always apparent or on the surface, our sense of self impacts on who and how we are at work. One of the study participants expressed this well, saying:

> . . . the most important thing you bring into your work is yourself.

(Quotes that appear in this book are taken from interviews with clinical educators by McAllister, 2001.) Having a sense of self includes having self-awareness and self-knowledge, self-acceptance and a self-identity, being aware of your level of need to control people, time and events, and seeing yourself as a life-long learner. A sense of self, although present in all participants, was less robust in the novice clinical educators. In part this was related to life stage development and general maturity levels, because the novices were young women not long out of university who were engaged in identity development in a range of life roles. However, targeted professional development can promote personal awareness and growth. Given the intense people focus of our work as clinicians and educators, and the humanistic orientation of our work as clinical educators, such professional development could be personally as well as professionally empowering for novice clinical educators. We suggest that interactions with students and learning from those experiences are powerful professional development opportunities for clinical educators.

A sense of relationship with others

Who you are as a person influences your sense of relationship with others, e.g. one of the participants in the McAllister (2001) study commented that she was:

> a collaborator in all aspects of my life – it's just me.

This theme includes being people oriented rather than self-oriented, perceiving others as they truly are not as we might wish them to be, holding personal values, and actively seeking to implement those values and perceptions in relating to others. The clinical educators in McAllister's (2001) study held a range of values including:

- Authenticity
- Trust
- Empathy and sensitivity
- Empowerment
- Mutuality.

They sought to implement these values in relationships through developing effective and empathic communication, and responding to students' emotional needs as well as their learning needs. The clinical educators involved in the study were prepared to put in the extra time and effort required to do their job well, and support others' development.

> [They] wanted to get to know the students as people and [understood] that takes time.

Relationship skills were highly developed in all the participants in the McAllister (2001) study, even in the novice clinical educators. Two factors appeared to contribute to this: the self-selection into health science courses of highly people-focused individuals, and the reinforcement and development of interpersonal skills in professional education. Clinicians typically graduate with excellent skills for working with clients and colleagues, and it seems to be relatively straightforward to transfer these skills to working with students. Nevertheless, working with marginal or failing students can challenge relationship and interpersonal skills (Maloney et al., 1997). Professional development can support the refinement of such skills and their maintenance under adverse conditions.

A sense of being a clinical educator

How you seek to relate to others influences your sense of being a clinical educator. This dimension includes understanding the types of roles adopted by clinical educators, motivations for becoming a clinical educator, having desired approaches to clinical education, and the emotional aspects of being a clinical educator. The desired approaches adopted by clinical educators in the study by McAllister (2001) included:

- Promoting the relevance of what students did to real world practice
- Being collaborative
- Having a plan for the placements
- Exercising control or allowing freedom for students
- Being flexible
- Balancing and juggling roles and responsibilities
- Promoting theory–practice integration
- Modelling life-long learning.

As with other aspects of being a clinical educator, approaches adopted change with experience and confidence in the role. In the absence of professional preparation for the role, novice clinical educators often simply adopt the approaches they experienced as students, with little understanding of the underpinning theory. However, even for experienced clinical educators, theory was only one factor guiding how they approached their work. Their desires to be true to themselves and to maintain empowering relationships with others in the workplace were equally important. They were essentially humanistic in focus, not managerial in orientation despite the influence of such approaches in the American clinical education literature (see, for example, Dowling, 2001). Professional development has an important role to play in helping clinical educators uncover and affirm their existing practice theory (see McAllister, 2002, for ways of doing this), as well as providing and extending appropriate educational theory.

A sense of agency

The fourth interlinked dimension arising from the McAllister (2001) study was sense of agency. Sense of agency encompasses both the areas on which a person acts and how confident and capable a person feels to take action; how clinical educators perceive their competence and capacity to act in terms of levels of skills and readiness, together with levels of confidence and comfort in the role are important elements of this dimension. The creation and maintenance of facilitative learning environments are important, as are designing, managing and evaluating students' learning programmes. Managing self and managing others were also key sub-themes in this dimension. This self- and other management was often directed towards containing possibly negative or relationship-damaging emotions and attitudes, as well as towards managing fatigue.

The essential structure of the first four dimensions of being a clinical educator was apparent in all participants in the study (McAllister, 2001); however, these dimensions were manifest in varying degrees dependent on experience. What distinguished the clinical educators in the study was the level to which they were able to achieve congruence between those dimensions.

Seeking dynamic self-congruence

Enabling a sense of self to be lived out authentically through relationships and actions in the workplace requires metacognitive and meta-mood monitoring. McAllister (2001) describes this dimension as one of seeking dynamic self-congruence, i.e. congruence between who one wants to be and who one actually is in the workplace. This involves bringing into play 'a higher level of awareness' (Torbert, 1978) to what you are doing, thinking and feeling, so that the selves (personal self, self in relationship and self as clinical educator) can be drawn together, in order to strive for action–plan congruence, i.e. congruence between what you plan to do and what you actually do.

The terms 'seeking' and 'dynamic' are important concepts in this dimension, because one cannot always achieve congruence; nor is achievement a steady-state phenomenon. It requires active cognitive and emotional awareness, and appears to be something that develops with experience in a role. Novice clinical educators are often too immersed in the moment and too self-focused, as they seek to survive in their new role, to have much spare processing capacity to give a higher level of attention to what they are about. They talk of their anxiety in their role and worry about completing all the roles and tasks required of them. Sustained high levels of attention are difficult to achieve, even for expert clinicians, because the complexity of the context, emotions and fatigue interferes with attention. Only when skills are deeply embedded in practice and you are able to be both self- and other focused, can high levels of awareness be sustained. We suggest that the ability to consistently achieve dynamic self-congruence is a hallmark of professional artists.

The final dimension to emerge in the McAllister (2001) study of the experience of being a clinical educator was one concerned with growth and development and is considered under the section of stages of development. Four stages of growth and development were identified. These are discussed below in the context of existing literature on growth and development in teachers and clinical educators in health professions.

Model 2: a model of the experience of being a speech–language pathology student in clinical education

As noted earlier this model is not derived from data, but rather adapted from model 1 which is grounded in research data developed with clinical educators. Our experience and intuition suggest that there are many parallels in the experience of being a student and a clinical educator. We suggest that the nature of the six dimensions in the experience of being a clinical educator would parallel those of being a speech–language pathology student in clinical education. Nevertheless, this model remains to be explored through a qualitative study of the experience of being a student learning in clinical contexts. The model is summarized in Table 1.7.

A sense of self

Learners need to develop a sense of self to become effective learners and clinicians. The self-awareness, self-knowledge, self-acceptance and self-identity that they begin to develop as students will continue to develop as clinicians, and hopefully as clinical educators of the future. A strong sense of self will assist students to establish their personal style in interactions with clients, peers and clinical educators, and to develop more easily a professional persona with which they are comfortable and which is facilitative for clients. In addition to this, we suggest that both clinical educators and students need to understand their relationship to and need

Table 1.7 Hypothesized dimensions and elements in the experience of being a student in clinical education

Dimension 1: a sense of self	Dimension 2: a sense of relationship with others
Elements	Elements
Having self-awareness and self-knowledge	Being people oriented
Having self-acceptance	Perceiving others
Having a self-identity	Values in relating to others
Understanding one's need for control vs freedom	Seeking to implement values and perceptions in relating to others
Being a life-long learner	

Dimension 3: a sense of being a learner	Dimension 4: a sense of agency as a learner
Elements	Elements
Understanding of role as learner	Perceptions of competence and capacity to act as a learner/student clinician
Understanding of role as student clinician	Assisting with creating and maintaining facilitative learning environments
Desired approaches to clinical education	Assisting with designing, managing and evaluating own learning programmes
Affective aspects of being a learner in clinical settings	Managing self
	Managing others

Dimension 5: seeking dynamic self-congruence	Dimension 6: growth and development – possible stages and pathways
Elements	Elements
Bringing a higher level of attention to the roles of learner and student clinician	Novice/beginner level student
Drawing the selves together	Intermediate level student
Striving for plan–action congruence	Competent/entry level student

From McAllister (2001)

for control versus freedom. This is particularly the case for students who will often need to accommodate to levels of control or freedom established by others for them.

A sense of self in relationship

We suggest that the elements of this dimension are the same as those for clinical educators. This is because both good clinical practice from students and good clinical education require attending to the needs of others and enacting humanistic values.

A sense of being a learner

The elements in this dimension would largely be the same as those for clinical educators, except that students probably come to clinical placements with one or two common motivations – to learn to be clinicians, or to 'pass' – as opposed to clinical educators who may have a range of motivations, as discussed earlier. Both parties need to understand their roles. Just as clinical educators have dual roles as educators and clinicians, students must embrace roles as learner *and* student clinician. Both parties will have desired approaches to clinical education. Although we have some insight into what these are for clinical educators, we can only surmise what these might be for students. Based on work by Chan et al. (1994) and Nemeth (2004) of students' perceptions and experiences of clinical education, we suggest that students hope that clinical placements:

- are well organized
- are flexible
- promote theory–practice integration
- are relevant to future practice
- permit them some measure of control over their learning
- enable them to juggle clinical education and other life, study, work commitments

and that their clinical educators will:

- recognize where they are in their growth
- help them manage their anxieties
- structure and support their learning
- develop a relationship of mutuality and collegiality.

As with clinical educators, students experience a range of emotions in their work and interactions in the clinical environment (Nemeth, 2004). Anxiety (Chan et al., 1994) and self-doubt are prominent emotions for students.

A sense of agency as a learner/student clinician

As with clinical educators, for students this dimension is concerned with confidence and capacity to act, and what is to be acted on. We suggest that students need to have or develop a sense that they can act to create supportive learning environments as well as be involved in designing, implementing and evaluating their learning programmes. If a goal of clinical education is to produce self-directing, self-evaluating graduates, then enabling students to develop the skills and confidence to act in these directions is important. Like clinical educators, students must learn to manage themselves, and others, effectively, especially their clinical educators. As we discuss in Chapter 4, the development of personal skills needed for the management of self and others is challenging for students, as indeed it is for clinical educators.

Seeking dynamic self-congruence

Like clinical educators, students too need to be able to be true to them-selves, live out personal values and achieve congruence between plans and actions. To achieve such personal and plan–action congruence requires the ability to be other focused and also to pay attention to one's own metacognition and emotional states. This is particularly challenging for students, as discussed in Chapter 4. Perhaps it is only at the compe-tent, and soon to be the entry level, that this can be realistically sought by students.

Growth and development

The pursuit of expertise and professional artistry are unrealistic goals for students. Instead we describe their development in terms of novice/begin-ner level, intermediate, and competent/entry level stages. These stages of student development are elaborated on more in the next section about stages of development.

The previous two models described the experience of being a clinical educator and a student. Although interaction between students and clin-ical educators is considered in those models, it is explicitly addressed in the next two models. Both models highlight the professional develop-ment required of students and clinical educators in order to be able to respond appropriately to student development.

Model 3: the Continuum of Supervision (Anderson, 1988)

The Continuum of Supervision has as its goal the production of inde-pendent clinicians capable of self-supervision. Anderson proposes three developmental stages in her continuum:

1. Evaluation–feedback stage
2. Transition stage
3. Self-supervision stage.

The horizontal lines in Figure 1.1 suggest the amount of talking and hence control assumed by the educator. In the evaluation–feedback stage, students have little skill and require clinical educators to use a dominant, direct/active style of supervision where they direct students' activities and provide most of the feedback. Students in the transitional stage are grad-ually becoming more clinically skilled and independent, taking more control and doing more talking in the form of self-evaluation, questioning and commenting to clinical educators. Clinical educators need to respond to this development in students by assuming a more collaborative style of supervision. This involves sharing responsibility for the design and management of the learning programme, establishment of client goals and programmes, and the provision of feedback. In the final stage, students and clinical educators work together in a peer–consultation relationship. This is characterized by students doing most of the initiating and talking, management of their learning programme and client programmes, and using clinical educators as consultants for largely independent learning and case management. Self-awareness, self-monitoring, active participation and joint decision-making are important features of this model. These features are consistent with Anderson's view that the goal of clinical education is personal and professional growth for both the student and the clinical educator.

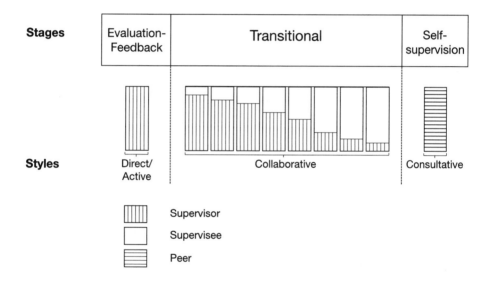

Figure 1.1 A Continuum of Supervision (adapted from Anderson, 1988).

Model 4: the Integrative Task–Maturity Model of Supervision (Mawdsley and Scudder, 1989)

Table 1.8 presents an adaptation of the Mawdsley and Scudder model, focusing on the maturity level and characteristics of students at different stages of professional development, and appropriate interactional responses from their clinical educators, which can help promote students' growth and development. Unlike the Anderson (1988) model, this model does not emphasize the dynamic nature of professional development for the clinical educator.

Table 1.8 An abridged and adapted version of the Integrative Task–Maturity Model of Supervision

Maturity level of student	Level 1	Level 2	Level 3	Level 4
	Not competent	Not competent	Competent	Competent
	Not confident	Confident	Not confident	Confident
	Not willing	Willing	Willing	Willing
Clinical educator style	Telling	Selling	Participating	Delegating

Adapted from Mawdsley and Scudder (1989)

Mawdsley and Scudder identify three attributes of students at increasingly more mature levels of professional development: competence, confidence and willingness. They suggest that students start their professional development as not competent, confident or willing. Appropriate interactions with their clinical educators would be focused on clinical educators telling students what to do and how to do it, i.e. providing a high degree of structure, so that students can gain some success with the task at hand and increased confidence. As confidence and therefore willingness to undertake tasks increase, perhaps initially without a concomitant increase in clinical competence, clinical educators can adopt different styles to support changing levels of competence and confidence.

The above discussion of models emphasizes the potential for parallel personal and professional development of students and clinical educators, and notes that both parties go through stages in their development. These stages are described in the next section.

Stages of professional development in clinical educators

Four stages of growth and development emerged from McAllister's (2001) study of clinical educators. These were labelled using terms borrowed from Dreyfus and Dreyfus (1986) and Benner (1984). An alternative pathway in professional life was also noted – that of burnout. As this is not a 'goal' of professional development in clinical educators, it is not discussed here, but is discussed in Chapter 4 as one consequence of a lack of development of personal and interpersonal skills.

The novice

Brammer (1996), in a study of nurse educators, noted that they described becoming a clinical educator as 'one big learning experience'. Novice clinical educators in the McAllister (2001) study also noted that experience.

They were anxious about their clinical education expertise and wary of having others observe them. Their sense of self as a competent person and clinician was challenged, and their self-esteem could be fragile. They feared:

> . . . having to explain what they were doing and why to others [i.e. students].

As with novice classroom teachers, they were self-focused – a finding supported by the work of Christie et al. (1985) with occupational therapy clinical educators. Clinical educators in McAllister's (2001) study role-modelled themselves as clinical educators (and possibly as clinicians) on others with whom they had worked, either as students or as colleagues in the current context. They were anxious about 'having enough time' and managing the daily clinical tasks. They may not have engaged in self-directed learning or actively sought support from colleagues. They were in what Katz (1972) called 'survival mode'.

The advanced beginner

One of the major tasks for clinical educators at this stage of development was 'getting comfortable' in their new role. They actively sought ways to decrease the anxiety they had experienced in moving into their new role. As a result, they became like the teachers studied by Glickman (1980) – more people focused and less self-focused. If they were reflective learners (see Chapter 6), they began to reflect more often on their performance and seek help from others in obtaining feedback or clarification of things of concern to them. They still did not know 'what was normal' or what to expect from the typical student. In other words, their store of patterns was not yet large and they could not use pattern recognition (see Chapter 5 for more information) as their major entrée into reasoning about educational issues. They could be quite controlling and felt responsible for the success or failure of clinical placements, a finding also noted by Christie et al. (1985). They slowly came to realize the impact that their sense of self had on the way they related to others in the educational context. They tried out new ways of being and doing and managing situations, attempting to individualize student learning programmes, but sometimes ended up with feelings of discomfort or frustration if things did not work out.

The competent practitioner

Competent clinical educators have achieved a level of expertise in their work. They have found ways that work for them, which produce effective outcomes for their students and clients, and for themselves. They were in what Katz (1972) refers to as a stage of consolidation. Their professional craft knowledge as clinical educators and their personal knowledge combined with their discipline knowledge to produce effective outcomes. They were able to 'look for the flow' in activities and interactions to determine the right timing for intervention. They were able to be both other focused and aware of and meet their own needs. Competent professionals are often highly people-focused individuals and they can use their interpersonal skills to influence outcomes. They can be flexible in accommodating the needs of others. As noted by Christie et al. (1985), competent clinical educators see themselves as resource people, facilitators and guides, rather than as people with all the answers, responsibility and control. They had the confidence to let go of some of their programme control. With these changed perceptions came a greater emphasis on supporting and nurturing students' individuality and creativity, allowing them greater responsibility and independence. There was a high degree of 'comfortableness' with the ways things were done.

Some competent clinical educators may choose, consciously or otherwise, to maintain this comfortable state and not seek to extend themselves. Others may draw on internal motivations and wish to aspire towards continued personal and professional growth. Sometimes, external forces, such as major changes in the clinical education programme or the experience of having to fail a student on placement, may create the imperative for growth and change. When competent clinical educators are able to bring a higher level of attention to their work and self-initiate further growth and development, we suggest that they are striving for professional artistry.

The professional artist

McAllister (2001) noted that professional artists in clinical education were those who brought a high level of self-knowledge and self-awareness to the clinical education role, recognizing that:

> . . . the most important thing you bring into your job is yourself.

They sought to be authentically themselves in the workplace, and they sought to live out their personal values in the workplace. They had very high levels of professional expertise but were also aware of areas that needed further improvement. They were not complacent about their achievements or skills and actively pursued improvement and excellence. They were 'open about their strengths and weaknesses' and able to accept criticism from colleagues. Like mature successful teachers in studies of teacher development, they were very other focused (Glickman, 1980) and sought opportunities for renewal (Katz, 1972). They used their interpersonal skills to 'talk things through and work things through' with others in the workplace. They were collaborative in their approach and sought to empower rather than control others. They were able to bring high levels of interpersonal and task-directed awareness to their roles, and multi-task with ease. They could work 'with one ear listening' to what else was going on around them, and identify the right moment for a timely intervention or supportive comment to those with whom they were working. They used their intuition and emotional intelligence (Goleman, 1995) to great effect.

Professional artists in the clinical education arena consistently strive for and more often achieve what we have referred to previously as dynamic self-congruence. Our work with clinical educators striving for professional artistry suggests that they are open to self-exploration and exploration by others of their knowledge, practice, values and thoughts. They also engage in reflective practices to promote their professional development. Many of the processes they use are the same as those used to promote growth and development by students.

Stages of development in students

Speech–language pathology students also pass through several stages of development on their journey towards entry level competency. By entry level competency we mean the expected levels of competency at students' points of graduation from their university courses. The next section describes some of the characteristics of novice, intermediate and entry level students. These descriptions are based on the small amount of literature that is available and our experiences in working with students at each of these levels.

The novice student

Students at the novice level are generally undertaking their first clinical placement in speech–language pathology. This stage is characterized by high levels of anxiety about interactions with clients (Chan et al., 1994). Students may be preoccupied with questions such as:

- Will the client like me?
- Will the client have confidence in me?
- Will I do the right thing? What will my clinical educator think?
- Will I remember everything?

As these questions indicate, students may be self-focused in that they are only concerned with how clients may impact on the students themselves.

Students at the novice level are also likely to be highly motivated to determine whether they have made a correct career choice and therefore may be enthusiastic learners who show a reasonable degree of self-direction (Ferguson and Fitzpatrick-Barr, 2001). Our experience is that novice students can be delightful to work with because of their enthusiasm, high levels of motivation and eagerness to learn.

Students at this level will require a high degree of support from their clinical educators in all aspects of client management, e.g. treatment plans may need to be discussed in detail before each session and reports may need to cycle through multiple drafts before they are of an acceptable standard. Clinical educators will also need to assist students to access or re-access theoretical bases, and help them to apply and interpret theory in relation to the clients with whom they are involved. Students at this level will require direct and active supervision (Anderson, 1988) in that they will need to be shown or told what and how to approach tasks, and they will need concrete and specific feedback about their performance. Novice students in clinical education will also take large amounts of time to prepare for client interactions and to produce accurate and acceptable documentation about clients. We have found that supervising novice level speech–language pathology students can be very rewarding because of the enormous gains they make in terms of their development of clinical skills, communication skills and professional skills in a short period of time.

The intermediate student

Students at this stage will vary in their level of competency depending on the complexity of the caseload with which they are working and the complexity of the workplace environment in which they find themselves. Generally students are able to begin to relate relevant theory to their clinical work and to plan for client management in consultation with their clinical educators. Students may need support from their clinical educators to assist them to view clients holistically and to engage in clinical reasoning processes. Intermediate level students are also able to focus on the client in interactions and the impact of their behaviours on the client. Students are able to reflect on their own performance after assessment or treatment sessions and begin to evaluate both positive and negative aspects of their performance. Students at this level are able to perform some routine clinical tasks well, e.g. making appointments and writing in files.

Clinical educators generally adopt a collaborative style of supervision when working with intermediate level students (Anderson, 1988). Students begin to bring their own ideas, observations and plans to the clinical educator who works with the student to complete the process. This may involve assisting students to prioritize tasks, goals or learning activities, complete the clinical reasoning process or accurately self-evaluate their performance.

The entry level student

Students at this level are able to perform most of their clinical work independently and competently. However, consultation or collaboration will be required for clients or situations that students have not previously experienced or if the caseload or workplace environment is sufficiently complex. Entry level students are able to use clinical reasoning skills to make decisions and solve problems, and they are able to prioritize information, goals and activities to ensure holistic client management. These students are able to apply theoretical knowledge to ensure that all aspects of practice are evidence based (Sackett et al., 2000).

At this stage of development clinical educators consult with students about concerns, queries or questions that students may bring to them. Clinical educators are also likely to play an important role in providing learning opportunities that will allow students to extend and test their skills. Chan et al. (1994) also found that students' levels of anxiety may increase as they prepare to finish their degrees and enter the workforce. Uncertainty about their 'preparedness' for the workforce and feelings of 'not knowing everything' appeared to be the basis for this anxiety (Chan et al., 1994).

Appendix 1.1: Goals of clinical education

- Understanding of health, illness and the healthcare system
- Awareness of own attitudes, values and responses to health and illness
- Ability to cope effectively with the demands of the professional role
- Understanding of the interrelated roles of the healthcare team
- Clinical competencies relevant to students' disciplines, including clinical reasoning skills, psychomotor competencies, and interpersonal and communication skills
- Ability to provide sound rationales for interventions/actions
- Skills in the education of relevant people (e.g. patients, clients, the community, staff)
- Self-management skills (e.g. time and workload management)
- Ability to evaluate critically and develop own performance
- Ability to review and investigate the quality of clinical practice
- Professional accountability and commitment to clients/self/employers
- Commitment to maintain and develop professional competence
- Skills necessary for life-long professional learning

- Ability to respond to changing community healthcare needs
- Readiness to work in complex, changing work environments
- Generic attributes
- Capability to deal with both familiar and unfamiliar circumstances
- Professional artistry
- Social responsibility
- Cross-cultural sensitivity and competence
- Cross-cultural communication skills
- Capacity to work in a range of settings (including primary health care, community-based rehabilitation, hospital settings, indigenous rural communities, overseas, etc.).

CHAPTER 2

Preparing for clinical education

Speech–language pathologists work in the volatile and constantly changing contexts of health and education. They are members of a profession that undergoes regular redefinition of roles, responsibilities, competencies and specializations (see, for example, recent 'scopes of practice' published by the Speech Pathology Association of Australia, 2002c and the American Speech–Language–Hearing Association, 2001). University professional preparation programmes in speech–language pathology aim to produce graduates who can operate successfully within an environment of constant change. One way that students are prepared is through clinical education experiences. Students work with clients in health and education settings at various stages during their professional preparation. Arguably, clinical education is the most influential and critical part of the preparation of future speech–language pathologists. Clinical placements are the way in which clinical education experiences are formalized, managed and assessed.

The 'teacher as manager' model (Romanini and Higgs, 1991) describes three stages of clinical placements: preparation, implementation and evaluation. This chapter takes a chronological approach to an in-depth discussion of the preparation stage. We begin by considering the issues involved in deciding whether to accept a student on placement. Planning for the placement and orienting students and clinical educators to the placement are then explored. Deciding on learning experiences through the use of learning contracts is also addressed. Reflections, challenges and checklists for the reader are presented throughout the chapter.

The 'teacher as manager' model

We have chosen to discuss this particular model in detail because it provides a comprehensive account of the stages that students and clinical educators pass through during the course of a placement. The model provides a structured way of thinking about the clinical education process in its entirety. Other models of clinical education (see Chapter 1) often describe a portion of the clinical education process, usually the implementation stage (Anderson, 1988; Brasseur, 1989; Mandy, 1989). Although those models are useful and insightful, for the purpose of this book we have elected to use the teacher as manager model as the framework for discussing methods in clinical education. The three stages identified in the teacher as manager model are described below.

The preparation stage

Romanini and Higgs (1991) describe six substages of the preparation stage: clinical educators' prior planning and preparation; initial encounter of clinical educators and students; preliminary exploration of learning goals and strategies; focus on area for learning; assessment of learner readiness; and preparatory activities. This stage consists of whatever occurs before the placement and the early contacts between students and clinical educators.

The implementation stage

Students and clinical educators move into the implementation stage when students are ready to start engaging in learning tasks. This stage includes the following substages: clarification and planning of learning goals and strategies; the learning experience; and ongoing review of progress with students.

The evaluation stage

McLeod et al. (1997) state that the evaluation stage involves 'clinical educators and students in evaluating the learning program and its outcomes and determining any subsequent action' (p. 49). This stage has four substages: evaluation of programme input, process and outcomes; application; the end; and entering a new cycle.

Within the teacher as manager model clinical educators have a number of roles to fulfil (see Chapter 3); however, clinical educators' overarching role is that of learning programme manager. A decision to accept students on placement is also a decision to take on the role of learning programme manager. The next section discusses issues to consider when thinking about whether or not to accept students on placement.

To take a student or not?

The decision to take students on clinical placement is not one that is made lightly. Potential clinical educators need to examine their motivations for accepting students on placements, their ability to manage a learning programme and the suitability of the site for student placements.

Motivation

Essentially, potential clinical educators need to assess and identify why they wish to take students on placement. Table 2.1 contains a summary of suggested reasons why clinicians may become clinical educators (adapted from Lincoln et al., 1997a).

Personal reflection: reflections on my motivations as a clinical educator

Look down the list in Table 2.1 and attempt to identify any of the motivations that may apply to you.

Table 2.1 Motivations of clinical educators

1	Continued learning
2	Professional and personal development
3	Career advancement
4	Develop or maintain links with universities
5	Update theoretical knowledge
6	To earn extra money
7	Gain a title (and status) such as 'student unit supervisor'
8	Enjoyment of interacting with beginning students as an advanced student
9.	Redress negative experiences they may have had as students
10	Required part of an academic position
11	Increase productivity of the service or department
12	Feel professionally obligated to take students
13	Pressure from universities to provide placements

Individuals' motivations will, to some extent, influence how they approach the task of clinical supervision, e.g. if a clinical educator's primary motivation is to redress his or her own negative experiences on clinical placements, he or she may approach the supervisory relationship with fixed ideas about how he or she will interact with students and may over-compensate for his or her own negative experiences. According to the model of being a clinical educator presented in Chapter 1 (McAllister, 2001), this clinical educator would be striving to achieve congruence between his or her clinical education practices and his or her sense of self and sense of relationship with others. If, however, a clinical educator's primary motivation is to increase the productivity of the department, he or she may not have considered how to interact with students, but may rather be focused on logistics and client care issues. So, it is important at the outset to be aware of self-motivation when considering taking students on placement. The following quotes are attempts by speech–language pathologists to articulate their motivations about accepting students on placement (McAllister, 2001):

> Students provide an updating, someone with whom to discuss ideas and get a new perspective on clients.

> I've always been interested in personal development and interested in people and how they develop, and combining that particular interest with the growth and development of the students is what interested me in clinical education.

> To be perfectly honest I didn't really have much choice but the uni rang up and begged for a placement; I probably would have left it a bit longer before I took students.

Ability to manage a learning programme

The teacher as manager model identifies five roles that clinical educators may adopt when becoming learning programme managers: task manager; group manager (if more than one student is being accepted on placement at one time); individual development manager; environment manager; and overall programme manager (Romanini and Higgs, 1991). These roles indicate that clinical educators: organize the practical aspects of the placement, e.g. access to clients, work space and equipment; facilitate the learning of individual students, e.g. assist students to set and achieve individual goals; facilitate and manage group dynamics; and are also responsible for meeting the requirements of the universities in terms of learning experiences and assessment procedures. Other authors have suggested that the roles of clinical educators may also include that of role-model, colleague, teacher, evaluator, administrator, counsellor and researcher (McLeod et al., 1997).

One way of thinking about the role of learning programme manager is that it requires an extension of the skills required on a daily basis within health and education settings, e.g. the skills used to run group interventions with clients may be similar to those required to ensure that students work in a collaborative, facilitative group. Similarly the negotiation and conflict resolution skills used when interacting with fellow team members are probably similar to those needed when negotiating and solving problems with students. The clinical and interpersonal skills that speech–

language pathologists are required to possess means that they are part-ially prepared for the role of learning programme manager.

Potential clinical educators must also familiarize themselves with the requirements and assessment procedures of the university. Most universi-ties offer written information on these topics or run regular workshops for new clinical educators. Below are further issues for clinical educators to consider in relation to their potential role of learning programme manager.

Personal reflection: reflections on my role as a clinical educator

- Do I have a clear understanding of the university's requirements?
- Do I have good organizational skills?
- Do I have ideas about where I want students to be at the end of the placement and how they might get there?
- Do I enjoy teaching?
- Am I enthusiastic about my profession and learning?
- Do I have time to manage students' learning programmes?

In our experience, clinical educators sometimes report that they are too busy to take on the role of learning programme manager. We have also found that these same people may report to us, at the end of a placement, that clinical education experiences have helped refresh and refocus their energy, and renew their interest in their chosen field. Some even report that sharing some of the workload with a student and focusing their skills on facilitating student learning reduced the stress associated with their normal workload. Below are some more comments from clinical educa-tors about having students on placement (McAllister, 2001):

> Seeing where a student is at and watching them grow as a clinician gives me pleasure in my work.

> Clinical education is a two-way process where both the student and I grow, where we both make mistakes, but hopefully learn from them.

> I enjoy the challenges because students keep you on your toes.

We also acknowledge that not all speech–language pathologists will enjoy being involved in clinical education and that there are times when, for logistical reasons, it is not possible for clinics to accept students on placement. Sometimes there is a time lag between when an offer for a placement is made and when a student arrives at the placement. In the meantime, circumstances change, making it not a good time to have a student, but the decision is made to go ahead anyway. In situations such as this, we suggest that clinical educators tell their students what the circumstances are and what factors may be causing stress for the site or clinical educators. Students can sense that things are 'not right' and it is better that they understand the real reasons rather than worry that they are the cause of difficulties or that they themselves are unwelcome.

Suitability of the site for student placements

Potential clinical educators also need to decide whether their workplace is conducive to student learning. Examples of questions clinical educators may ask are:

• Is there sufficient space to accommodate students?
• Is it legally and ethically appropriate for students to be on placement at this site?
• Can a range of appropriate clinical experiences be provided?

If you are unsure about the suitability of your site for student placements, you might discuss your concerns with the person responsible for clinical placements at the university. Student placements also need to have the support of colleagues, other team members, senior staff and clients. General support at the clinical site is necessary to ensure that the students are accepted and welcomed into the department and that clinical educators receive support from their managers and colleagues. Below is one of the many challenges that clinical educators may face in their workplace; other challenges are presented throughout this book and it is advisable to take the time to consider the opportunities that each challenge may afford in terms of personal and professional growth for the clinical educator and the students.

Learning exercise 2.1: accepting students on placement during times of organizational change (Add your own ideas to the list of advantages and disadvantages below.)

Advantages
Student may have an outsider's perspective, experience from other clinical settings, may allow regular clinical services to be provided while you give thought to the changes required . . . .

Disadvantages
Ground rules and procedures may not be clearly developed and documented for students to follow, clinical educators' feelings about change may be negative, stress levels may be higher . . . .

The nature of contemporary practice in speech–language pathology is such that change is the only constant. Potential clinical educators may need to think creatively and laterally about what a 'suitable' placement may be. Arguably, if new graduates will be faced with constant change in their workplaces, then we must also provide clinical experiences in climates of transition and change.

To go on a placement or not?

Before moving on to a discussion of the early phases of a learning programme, it is worthwhile at this point to consider briefly students' motivations in accepting clinical placements. At the most fundamental level students go on clinical placements to fulfil the requirements of their academic degree. Students may also be motivated to experience their profession in 'the real world' or to apply the theory they have learnt at university. Other students may have requested a particular placement because it will give them experience in an area they want to work in or it fills in a gap in their clinical experiences to date. Some students may seek particular placements because they are known to be challenging and rewarding (Lincoln et al., 1997a).

Other less learning-oriented motivations could include: the location of the placement site is close to home; the placement dates fit in with part-time work arrangements; or the clinical educator at the site is known to be 'student friendly'. Unfortunately some students go on placements because there are no others available to choose from or they do not have a choice. When this occurs students may need to be assisted to see the learning experiences that the placement may afford them. Just as it is important to be aware of your motivations when accepting students on placement, it is helpful to ask students about theirs. Although it is unlikely that students will freely admit to motivations that are not learning oriented, clear communication about learning-oriented motivations by students can assist clinical educators in their assessment of the suitability of their site for placements and in the early planning of the placement, e.g. if a student states that his or her motivation in accepting a placement is to gain experience with a particular type of communication disorder, the clinical educator may ensure that this occurs by making arrangements during the planning stage of the placement.

Pre-placement planning

This section considers pre-placement planning, both personal and organizational, by clinical educators. It also discusses ways in which clinical educators can assist students' pre-placement planning and preparation.

Clinical educators

As it is likely that some organizational and personal preparation will be required, clinical educators need to begin planning for student placements well in advance. If it is the first time students have been accepted

Table 2.2 Issues for clinical educators to consider during pre-placement planning

Pre-placement planning

Task manager
1. Investigate availability of learning experiences (this may involve consulting other team members and colleagues in your own and other professions, and analysing your own caseload, workload and future activities)
2. Create learning experiences, think about broad and specific clinical skills (this may be your chance to get a project off the ground!)
3. Gain cooperation of other staff members in providing learning experiences
4. Decide in which tasks students can and cannot be involved, and what levels of supervision tasks will require (this may need to be done in consultation with others and with reference to the policies and procedures of your workplace)

Group manager
5. Explore ways of grouping and ungrouping students (through observation of group dynamics)
6. Decide which tasks will be best completed in a group or pair and which ones should be completed by students individually
7. Think about the implications of groups and pairs for assessing students individually

Individual development manager
8. Ensure that you are clear about the level of experience of each student who is coming and the expectations for the placement
9. Think about how you can assist students to meet these expectations
10. Decide how will you know if students are progressing satisfactorily
11. Know what to do if progress is not satisfactory

Environment manager
12. Organize space for the students to work in
13. Let other staff members know in advance the dates of the placement, the names of the students and their level of expertise
14. Prepare appropriate orientation materials and experiences (see below)
15. Organize name tags, security clearances, parking, etc.

Overall programme manager
16. Read placement material provided by the university
17. Read your own notes and reflections and goals from previous placements
18. Think about your goals for this placement
19. Revise clinical education research and theories
20. Develop a vision about how you would like the placement to progress

at the clinical site or it is a clinical educator's first time supervising, then pre-placement planning will be even more vital to the success of the placement. Novice clinical educators have reported to us that developing daily, weekly and possibly monthly timetables helps to reassure them that it is possible to fit in all the demands of the placement and their regular workload. Table 2.2 presents a checklist aimed at highlighting issues for consideration by clinical educators in the preparation stage. The issues have been grouped according to the various roles the clinical educator is required to fulfil in the teacher as manager model.

McAllister's (2001) model also suggests that clinical educators may benefit from reflection on their own sense of self and sense of relationship with others before the start of placements (see Chapter 3). In particular, novice clinical educators may reflect on their need to control people, time and events, whereas experienced clinical educators may choose to reflect on their view of themselves as a life-long learner. Clinical educators may also reflect on and evaluate a professional relationship that is problematic for them, in order to get in touch with their sense of relationships with others. Doing this may highlight aspects of human relationships that are important and those that are not for us as individuals.

Students

There are several potential ways to assist students in their planning and preparation for placements. The goal here is to begin facilitating students' learning before they start their placement. Some clinical educators find it helpful to send students information about the placement site in advance. This might include information about the caseload, types of learning experiences available, context of the placement site, a reading list, a list of the tests/equipment/instrumentation at the placement, and contact details. Other clinical educators find a pre-placement visit a few weeks before the placement starts helps students to prepare. For clinicians in rural and/or remote areas a lengthy phone conversation or interaction via email may be suitable. This type of pre-placement activity gives students a clear message that they are expected to do some preparation before the start of the placement. It also allows students to focus their preparation and thereby prepare more efficiently.

Students themselves need to review their goals from previous placements and think about new ones for the new placement. They may need to work on their motivation levels and prepare both intellectually and emotionally. Students may also need to investigate practicalities such as transport, accommodation, financial issues, equipment purchasing and resource gathering before starting the placement. Some of the overlapping preparatory activities of students and clinical educators are summarized in Table 2.3.

Table 2.3 Preparation for clinical educators and students

Clinical educators	Students
Identify motivations for accepting students on placement	Identify motivations for accepting the clinical placement
Why am I taking this student now?	Why do I want a placement at x?
Identify attitudes towards students and expectations of students and their universities	Identify attitudes towards and expectations of the site, caseload, clinical educator
What are my attitudes towards students at this level of experience?	What am I thinking about working with this type of client?
Familiarize self with placement requirements	Familiarize self with placement requirements
Do I know what to expect and what is expected?	Do I know what is expected of me on this placement?
Investigate and create learning experiences	Identify learning experiences they would like to obtain.
What can this placement offer students?	What gaps in experience do I have?
Prepare other team members for the placement	Investigate who the other members of the team are and their respective roles
Are others aware that students will be here?	Am I aware of the roles of each team member?
Prepare/revise orientation materials	Read and participate in orientation activities
What do the students need to know to operate effectively in this environment?	What areas am I still unclear about?
Set goals for themselves for the placement	Set goals for themselves for the placement
What aspects of my clinical education skills do I want to improve?	What aspects of my clinical skills do I want to improve?

Orienting students

Experienced clinical educators report that a thorough orientation of students to the placement site is time-consuming initially, but saves time later during the placement. It is likely that students who are well oriented to the physical layout, organizational policy, management structures and requirements of clinical educators will develop independence at a greater rate than those who are not.

Orientation involves familiarization with personnel and organization of the placement site, as well as rapport building and information exchange between students and clinical educators. During this process students begin refining the learning goals that they have brought with them and adapting them to the setting, and clinical educators begin to develop rapport with students and to gauge their current level of knowledge and skills. In our experience it is helpful if students and clinical educators share some information about their interests outside of work as part of the rapport building process. Vignette 2.1 illustrates how a talented clinical educator used information about a student's interests to help her bring more of her own personality and personal style into her developing professional persona.

Vignette 2.1: using rapport to empower students

A clinical educator discovered through chatting with a shy and somewhat withdrawn student that the student was a talented violinist. The clinical educator encouraged the student to give lunchtime recitals for clients and staff, which helped build the student's confidence and eased the student into the clinical environment. The clinical educator also allowed the student to use her music as a way of working successfully with a very difficult client who also loved music.

Orientation information and activities will vary between placement sites. It is helpful for students if all the information is located in a central place and an orientation timetable is provided for the first few days of the placement. Table 2.4 gives some suggestions for ways of generating ideas about the types of information to include in an orientation manual and suitable activities for students during the early days and/or weeks of the placement.

Table 2.4 Suggestions for developing content for an orientation manual

Brainstorm with colleagues

Ask other professionals how they orient students

Review orientation materials given to new staff members at your institution

Ask students about what sorts of things they have found helpful

Ask students for feedback at the end of the placement about what was most and least useful during orientation

Look at the student orientation manuals of other institutions, if possible

List materials, resources, equipment, etc. that you use frequently

List any handouts, guidelines, protocols, forms, etc. that you use frequently

Towards the end of the orientation process and as students start clinical work, clinical educators and students usually begin to negotiate about students' learning experiences. Again, a thorough orientation process will allow the student to develop realistic expectations about the learning goals that can be achieved during the placement.

Deciding on learning experiences

In this context we are using the term 'learning experiences' in its broadest sense. 'Learning experiences' refers not only to the tasks students will be engaged in but also to how they will learn in that context, what the clinical educators' roles will be in facilitating learning and how success in conducting the task will be defined and assessed.

The process of negotiating learning experiences usually begins with clinical educators describing the potential learning experiences that are available to students and the students subsequently presenting their learning goals for the placement. Clinical educators and students then work to match the learning experiences available to students' learning goals. Students and clinical educators negotiate whether the goals are feasible and achievable within the timeframe of the placement and the constraints of the clinical context. At this point the negotiations usually proceed into the realm of 'how' the goals will be achieved. Topics that might be discussed, clarified and negotiated could be the clinical educator's preferred supervisory style (Joshi, 1999), the student's preferred mode of receiving feedback, the learning processes that the student will employ, the level of supervision required, the level of supervision the clinical educator feels comfortable with, and the clinical educator's and student's learning styles.

Learning contracts

A useful way of documenting the decisions made about learning experiences is through the use of a learning contract or agreement. Learning contracts are a way of mapping the essential learning processes that must occur to achieve learning goals (Ladyshewsky, 1995). Contracts or agreements can be a way of 'exploring needs, establishing goals, dividing responsibilities and evaluating learning . . . [they] can also be supportive and reassuring in spelling out the expectations each has of each other' (Lincoln et al., 1997a, p. 75). Some generic features of learning contracts are learning goals, a plan for how the goals will be achieved, a timeframe for achievement, how the goals will be measured and assessed, responsibilities of the people involved in the contract and a mechanism for reviewing the contract after a specified period (Boud, 1992; Laycock and Stephenson, 1994).

Appendix 2.1, at the end of the chapter, contains an example of a learning agreement that is used by speech–language pathology students from the University of Sydney during their off-campus placements. Learning contracts are not a static document. Rather they can be reviewed and adjusted regularly to reflect changes in the placement such as the students' increasing competence, changes in supervisory needs or changes in the caseload or learning opportunities available.

Learning exercise 2.2: when learning contracts need to be re-negotiated

Sometimes students will not perform as well as expected on clinical placements and it may be necessary to re-negotiate the learning experiences in which they are going to be involved. Usually this occurs with a view to lightening students' workloads and removing some of the more difficult tasks. How can this be done, while ensuring that students are involved in a range of interesting experiences and do not experience a loss of confidence and motivation?

Learning contracts and clinical educators

Clinical educators may also make learning contracts with their managers or mentors or a personal learning contract with themselves. A contract may specify a clinical educator's learning goals for the placement period and how these may be achieved and assessed. The process of developing the contents of contracts may help clinical educators focus on their learning needs and facilitate them to develop new skills or to extend previously established skills. Bringing a higher level of attention to the development of skills in clinical education is one way that professional artistry in this area can be achieved, as discussed in Chapter 1, e.g. a clinical educator may contract with him- or herself to try to take a less directive approach with students (Joshi, 1999). The achievement of this goal might be measured by comparing the amount of clinical educator talk time with student talk time (Anderson, 1988; Kenny, 1996; Joshi, 1999) during discussions at the beginning, middle and end of the placement.

Clinical educators may also contract with students. A clinical educator may agree to attempt to use a different type of feedback with a student or to change his or her supervisory style. The achievement of these goals may be measured through the student's written or verbal feedback to the clinical educator. The use of learning contracts provides a powerful role-model to students of ways in which professional and personal growth can continue after graduation.

Conclusion

The 'teacher as manager model' (Romanini and Higgs, 1999) provides an overarching structure for clinical placements and may be particularly helpful for novice clinical educators to raise awareness of the many roles that clinical educators assume during placements. The model also highlights the importance of pre-placement planning and thorough orientation of students to the clinical education process. Chapter 3 discusses in detail the implementation phase of the teacher as manager model, and ways that students and clinical educators can learn together are explored in detail.

Appendix 2.1: Example of learning contract format for use by students and clinical educators

The University of Sydney
School of Communication Sciences and Disorders

Learning agreement between student and clinical educator for year 3 three-week adult clinic placements

Student name:_____Dates of placement:_____

Notes for completion by the student

This Agreement is to be completed after discussion and negotiation of all relevant areas by student and clinical educator. Should be completed by mid-week 1, and a *copy forwarded* to the **Director of Clinical Education** by *end week 1* of the placement.

Part A

Policies and procedures of the clinic/hospital
- Discussed and explained at orientation or day 1   ☐ Yes
- Policies and procedures manual provided by
  clinical educator at orientation or day 1   ☐ Yes

File notes/reports
- Formats and expectations discussed and example provided
- File notes to be completed what period of time after client contact?
  (Specify here) _____
- Reports to be completed what period of time after client contact?
  (Specify here) _____

Preference for supervision
• Discussed and points agreed as follows:

_____
_____
_____
_____
_____

Observation by student   ## Observation of student
(the amount and timing will change across the placement)

Negotiated in week 1	❑	Yes	Negotiated in week 1	❑	Yes
Re-negotiated in week 2	❑	Yes	Re-negotiated in week 2	❑	Yes
Re-negotiated in week 3	❑	Yes	Re-negotiated in week 3	❑	Yes

Feedback
(the type, amount and timing will change across the placement)

Negotiated in week 1 ❑ Yes
Re-negotiated in week 2 ❑ Yes
Re-negotiated in week 3 ❑ Yes

Self-evaluation activities to be undertaken by student, e.g. videoing, journalling
1.   Date:
2.   Date:
3.   Date:

To be shared with CE? or private use only?

Assessment of student clinical performances
To be completed mid-placement by CE only or CE and student (delete one)
To be completed end of placement by CE only or CE and student (delete one)

Part B

Clients to be worked with (initials only), swallowing/communication diagnosis/disorder, nature of contact (Ax, Rx, etc. please describe), frequency of contact (once a week, every day, etc.). Note no more than 3 hours of client contact per day, by end of placement.
•
•
•
•
•

Learning experiences that will be undertaken during the placement are (student to describe and identify as per CBOS)

1.

Which staff to consult or work with?

Comments on completion   Date of completion:

2.

Which staff to consult or work with?

Comments on completion   Date of completion:

3.

Which staff to consult or work with?

Comments on completion   Date of completion:

4.

Which staff to consult or work with?

Comments on completion   Date of completion:

Which staff to consult or work with?

Comments on completion   Date of completion:

Clinical educator signature: _____

Name of clinic: _____

Student signature: _____

Date of:
Initial agreement: _____

Completion of agreement: _____

Clinical educator (signature): _____

Student signature: _____

Date of completion of agreement: _____

CHAPTER 3

Learning together

Students 'need to learn' from their clinical educators in order to pass their assessments on clinical placements, as well as to become qualified, safe professionals. Clinical educators 'can choose to learn' from their students. In Chapter 1 we argued that participation in clinical education provides opportunities for both students and clinical educators to learn. There is much for both parties to learn in the clinical setting, and much they can learn from and with each other. Ideally, learning will occur together, as a result of a mutually supportive learning relationship, actively created and maintained by both the clinical educator and the student. This chapter discusses what we can learn from each other, and considers factors that contribute to the development of learning relationships in clinical education. We then discuss problems that may arise in learning relationships and some strategies for managing them.

Learning as a mutual exchange between clinical educator and student

Becoming a health professional is essentially about becoming someone who can successfully manage a range of relationships: with clients, their families, colleagues, other professionals, managers and students. In fact, as noted by Goodfellow et al. (2001), 'crucial moments in becoming a professional are often couched in terms of successful or unsuccessful relationships with others' (p. 161). The move to client-centred/patient-centred care, where the establishment of relationships with clients allows individualized and sensitive assessments of and responses to their needs, only seeks to highlight a long-established maxim of healthcare: that we do things 'with people' not 'to them'.

Among the array of professional relationships that students form during their years of professional preparation, probably the most crucial are those with their clinical educators. Not only do clinical educators provide clinical placements and support the development of students' knowledge and skill, but they also shape the development of personal and professional attributes in students through the role-models that they provide of professional and personal behaviour (McLeod et al., 1997). In addition, clinical educators have the power to 'make or break' students' emerging self-identities as professionals, as well as their personal self-esteem and confidence (Nemeth, 2003).

Just as clinical educators can have an enormous impact on student learning and personal and professional growth, so too can students have an enormous impact on their clinical educators. Students can provide affirmation of clinical educators' personal and professional skills, and challenges for personal and professional growth, and share knowledge and skills. Although the power differential is skewed in the direction of clinical educators, and they have the potential to do more harm to students than vice versa, relationships in the clinical education context that go awry can also damage the self-image and confidence of clinical educators, as clinicians, educators and people (McAllister, 2001).

Regardless of the outcomes of clinical placements, learning of one form or another will take place for both parties. Clinical educators will grow and learn as the result of affirming experiences, or from ones that create anxiety and self-doubt, such as those where students are failing. Students will also learn and grow as the result of their relationships with clinical educators, even those that lead to less than optimal learning environments or even failure. What is the nature of this learning and growth that occurs in the context of learning relationships?

What can we learn from each other?

The goals of learning are typically discussed in terms of knowledge, skills and attributes. For students, the learning goals of clinical education, such as those listed in Chapter 1, are often more clear cut, and can be readily grouped under such headings. The goals of learning for clinicians are typically couched in terms of increased knowledge and skills, in the pursuit of clinical expertise (see, for example, Benner, 1984). However, Fish and Coles (1998) have challenged traditional conceptualizations of what knowledge and skills matter, in their discussions of the development of professional judgement and professional artistry. In Chapter 1, we outlined goals for learning for clinical educators that are additional to those derived from traditional views of knowledge and skills. In the next section, we address three sets of skills needed to achieve these goals. These skills can be developed or extended in the context of clinical educators and students learning together.

Professional knowledge and skills

Students hopefully come to clinic with a solid base of theoretical or propositional knowledge. One of the goals of clinical education is to transform this propositional knowledge into what Higgs and Titchen (2000) call professional craft knowledge, i.e. the clinical 'know how' of 'how to get things done effectively and efficiently in the real world of clinical practice'. Clinical educators can help students develop this professional craft knowledge. They can assist students to develop their clinical reasoning by discussing with their students *why* they do things, as well as telling and showing *how* they do things in clinical settings. They can model clinical reasoning for their students by thinking aloud, as well as formally explicating reasoning, and inviting their students to ask questions that will help surface the practical and personal knowledge that underpins clinical expertise (see Chapter 5).

For clinical educators, participating in clinical education can afford many professional development opportunities. Clinical educators describe how students provide clinical educators informal opportunities for 'an updating, someone with whom to discuss ideas and get a new perspective' and they talk of how students 'keep you on your toes' (McAllister, 2001). Students can bring with them, from the university, the latest in techniques and propositional (theoretical) knowledge. If clinical educators are open to learning with and from their students, and see clinical education as an opportunity for professional growth for both parties, students and clinical educators can together work out how to transform this into professional craft knowledge. Accepting students may also offer clinical educators access to more formalized professional development opportunities through seminars and workshops run by the universities, and in some cases access to support for the conduct of research and clinical service development.

Personal knowledge and skills

Personal as well as professional growth should be an outcome for both clinical educators and students, according to Anderson (1988). Certainly, long-term, successful clinical educators acknowledge that being in an educator relationship with students affords opportunities for personal growth. McAllister (2001) found that clinical educators spoke of how they had become clinical educators because they had:

> . . . always been interested in personal development and interested in people and how they develop, and combining those particular interests is what interested [them] regarding the personal and professional growth of the students.

They commented that 'we both make mistakes but we both grow too'. Some confronted their 'need to be liked' and to 'please people' generally; others confronted their 'need to be in control'. One commented that she had learned with experience in the role that she 'could listen to negative feedback and that [her] world would not fall apart'. Another learned the value of conflict and confrontation, talking of 'pushing [her] student off the treadmill', rather than allowing the student to continue with unproductive learning and clinical behaviours.

The clinical education relationship offers students opportunities to try out and develop a range of personal attributes. Some of these attributes will already be part of students' emerging professional personas, based on personal and family values and attributes. Others may be role-modelled on lecturers and clinical educators with whom they interact. Clinical educators provide powerful role-models (McLeod et al., 1997) of values such as compassion, caring, and the pursuit of equity and justice for clients, as well as valuing life-long learning.

Life-long learning skills

One of the goals of contemporary higher education is to produce graduates who are life-long learners (Candy et al., 1994), as discussed in Chapter 1. Through their academic and clinical experiences, students hopefully are socialized into an expectation that they will continue to learn for the rest of their professional lives. A life-long learner can be defined as:

> . . . someone aware of what they know and can do, who is sensitive to the gaps in their professional skills and takes responsibility for seeking out opportunities to address their professional (and personal) development needs. In addition, they are enthusiastic about learning in all areas of life, take pleasure in helping others learn and reap considerable personal and professional satisfaction from seeing others grow personally and professionally. Life-long learners have a particular interest in understanding and achieving their potential and helping others identify and achieve theirs.
>
> McAllister (2001, p. 116)

Successful clinical educators see themselves as life-long learners (McAllister, 2001). They talk of their 'passion for learning', their 'thirst for knowledge', their 'enjoyment of instructing and helping others learn'. They also comment on how having students gives them 'an opportunity to put on another hat' – to wear an educator hat as well as a clinician hat – and reduces the 'isolation and stagnancy' of being a sole clinician. Having students provides them with stimulation and diversity in their professional lives. Students and clinical educators working together in learning relationships can promote and reinforce each other's moves to become life-long learners.

Building learning relationships

Building learning relationships requires a supportive environment, effective clinical teaching and learning skills, and good communication and interpersonal skills in both clinical educators and students.

A supportive environment

An environment supportive of the establishment and maintenance of a learning relationship in the clinical education setting would include adequate resources, forward planning and organization, a welcoming environment, peer support, and realistic shared expectations and understanding about the clinical education placement and processes. Well-managed learning programmes such as those discussed in Chapter 2 are likely to provide supportive learning environments.

Adequate resources

For a learning relationship to be maintained and learning goals to be achieved, there need to be enough tests, materials, stationery, desks, access to phones, Internet and library services, access to a tearoom, and personal storage space for students and clinical educators. Departmental colleagues can get annoyed if they feel that students are consuming scarce resources and space, and clinical educators need mental and physical space of their own where they can continue non-student-related tasks and regroup their thoughts. Students also need privacy, and to feel that they are not a drain on departmental resources. Table 3.1 contains a checklist of possible resources speech–language pathology students may need on placement.

Table 3.1 Checklist of resources for students

Desk and chair

Secure storage space for personal belongings

Storage space for journals, resources, etc.

Telephone and fax

Policies and procedures manual

Stationery

Access to assessment and treatment materials and clinical equipment

Access to a computer and printer

Access to Internet/email

Access to client files and the organization's record-keeping system

Parking

An organized placement

Student learning outcomes will be more successful, and the placement less stressful for all concerned when it is well organized. Clinical educators need to see themselves not only as educators but also as managers of students' learning programmes. Romanini and Higgs (1991) have advocated that clinical educators see themselves as teacher–managers. This involves management tasks in the preparation, implementation and evaluation of students' learning programmes, as outlined in Chapter 2. When things are flowing well and stress is reduced for students and clinical educators, it is more likely that an effective learning relationship can be developed.

Being welcome!

The demand for placements means that sometimes students are an unwanted burden on departments. Nevertheless, once a student has been accepted on placement, all staff as well as their clinical educators need to make students feel welcome. If factors such as staff shortages, departmental reorganizations, lack of space, increased workloads, illness or personal circumstances of staff make it difficult for students to be on site, but are explained, students can be reassured and adapt to less than ideal situations. Students can tell the difference between busy departments with clinicians that welcome them but must nevertheless get on with other duties, and those that resent having students. Not feeling welcome can be damaging to personal and professional growth and performance, as Vignette 3.1 shows.

Vignette 3.1: an example of a student who did not feel welcome

Erin, a final year speech–language pathology student, describes the damage to her self-esteem and confidence, and performance when she felt that she was not 'welcomed' by her clinical educator.

> I know they were really busy, but they just didn't 'welcome' me. I'm sure they didn't want me there. They didn't take me around and show me the hospital and didn't introduce me to other staff. They just left me in an office on my own. I was never involved in activities or morning tea. Apart from giving me my client list, the only time my clinical educator ever spoke to me was when I initiated it. I felt very unwelcome, as if I was a nuisance. Then he would give me short, usually negative feedback after I had seen a client. The first time he initiated contact was when he came to tell me at mid-placement that I was failing. This placement really damaged my self-confidence and my view of myself as an emerging clinician.

Similarly, clinical educators need to feel that they are valued and appreciated, that students really want to be on placement with them. Students won't always get the placements of their choice, but as Alsop and Ryan (1996) advise: 'There can actually be advantages to students having what they might consider to be a "less than ideal" placement' (p. 57). It can force students to extend their knowledge and skills in unanticipated ways, and promote flexibility, professionalism and clinical reasoning.

Peer support

It is well recognized that students learn better and more easily if they can work with peers (Lincoln and McAllister, 1993). Clinical educators also find having more than one student at a time on placements less stressful and more productive (Callan et al., 1994). It is less well recognized that clinical educators perform better and with less anxiety in their role as clinical educators if they also have the support of peers (McAllister, 2001). Lack of preparation and support of clinical educators is a chronic problem in the health sciences (Anderson, 1988; Best and Rose, 1996). However, novice clinical educators need this support to embark on and develop in the role (Christie et al., 1985; Brammer, 1996). Experienced clinical educators also need peer support to debrief and to manage challenging students.

Realistic and shared expectations

Clinical educators often tell us that universities do not clearly convey to them the universities' expectations for students on placements, and do not consult with sites about the appropriateness of expectations of students relative to what can be offered at the site or by the clinical educators. Inadequate briefing of students heading off on placements can compound this. Students may also bring to placements unrealistic expectations of the site or the clinical educators. Students may want more than can realistically be offered by a site or achieved in a placement. Further, in spite of adequate briefing, clinical educators sometimes develop unrealistic expectations of students or a mismatch of expectations with those of the university. This problem can be compounded when sites and clinical educators take students from more than one university.

Clearly, establishing clear communication and consistent expectations between all stakeholders is important to the establishment and maintenance of successful learning relationships. All parties have a role in ensuring that they clearly convey their expectations and understand those of other stakeholders. For your reference, appendices A, B and C in Anderson (1988) provide checklists for use by students to assist in understanding their expectations, needs and attitudes towards clinical supervision. These could be adapted for use by clinical educators, to form a platform for discussion by both parties at the start of a clinical placement. Even if such formal tools are not used, as a minimum standard universities should encourage their clinical educators and students to review needs, expectations, rights and responsibilities at the start of a placement, as part of orientation and goal-setting discussions. Students and clinical educators can prepare for this sharing of expectations and needs by considering the questions in the learning exercises below.

Learning exercise 3.1 (for students): what are your expectations of your clinical educator?

- List the expectations you hold for your clinical educator in your next placement.
- Now, ask yourself whether these are realistic expectations.
- If any seem unrealistic but you truly believe that you need these to be met to support your learning, what strategies can you use to seek to have these expectations met?

Clinical educators often hold many unspoken expectations about students. It helps to articulate these so you can assess whether or not they are realistic, and what you can do to ensure that important expectations are conveyed and met by students. What do you expect of students coming to you on placement? Do the exercise on your own or with colleagues. Are there discrepancies between their expectations and yours?

Learning exercise 3.2 (for clinical educators): what do you expect of students coming to you on placement?

- List the attitudes and behaviours you expect students to demonstrate on placement.
- Are these realistic? Achievable?
- How will you manage if these are not demonstrated?

Now compare your list with that compiled by Alsop and Ryan (1996), which appears in Table 3.2.

Effective teaching and learning skills

The characteristics of effective clinical teachers were deduced from a meta-analysis conducted by Edwards (1996) of previous studies of clinical educators in medicine and the health professions (Stritter et al., 1975;

Table 3.2 Expectations for students on placement

Students will:

Come well prepared for the placement, having read up about the conditions they might expect to see

Behave and dress according to the conventions of the service

Engage in the placement and take advantage of the learning opportunities that it offers

Demonstrate a commitment to learning and professional development

Take responsibility for their learning, engaging in reflection and honest self-evaluation of their performance and behaviour

Be punctual for appointments, and keep other people informed of difficulties

Integrate into the service team and respect the needs of its members

Take responsibility according to the stage of their training, but acknowledge the limits of their responsibility and experience so as not to endanger themselves or other people

Work in accordance with the Code of Ethics, and other standards of practice

Be inquisitive, and demonstrate an enquiring mind, and that they are prepared to develop a repertoire of skills and knowledge, using the resources available

Adapted from Alsop and Ryan (1996, pp. 58–59)

Irby, 1986; Hewson and Jensen, 1990; Stengelhofen, 1993; Price and Mitchell, 1993). Edwards suggested that such characteristics could be grouped into three major categories: teaching style, content of teaching and focus of the process. These categories of characteristics are shown in Table 3.3.

Table 3.3 Summary of characteristics of effective clinical teachers

Teaching style	Content of teaching	Focus of process
Fosters active student participation	Emphasizes applied problem-solving and critical appraisal skills	Promotes professionalism
Has a positive attitude to teaching	Extends knowledge and promotes its application	Provides professional support and encouragement
Has a range of teaching styles	Promotes skill development	Provides good clinical and professional role-model
Provides structure for learning/logically structured	Gives feedback on students' performance	
Provides intellectual challenge	Emphasizes references and research results	Optimizes patient care
Uses student-centred instruction; extensive interaction		
Has a humanistic orientation		

Adapted from Edwards (1996)

These categories of characteristics of effective clinical teachers form a useful evaluation benchmark. They can be used, by students and clinical education programme managers, to evaluate clinical educators. Clinical educators can also use them for self-evaluation.

Learning exercise 3.3: evaluation of self as an effective clinical educator.

- How would you rate yourself against the characteristics listed in Table 3.3?
- Which ones do you possess already?
- Which ones do you emphasize?
- Which ones might you need to develop?

Many of these effective teaching behaviours can be learned through professional development courses run by universities for their clinical educators, at either workshop, not-for-credit level, or as part of postgraduate qualifications. Professional associations such as the Royal College of Speech and Language Therapists and the Speech Pathology Association of Australia will count participation in clinical education workshops towards continuing professional development or registration requirements.

The section above outlines some of the characteristics of effective clinical teachers. What might be some of the characteristics of effective clinical learners? In part they relate to the expectations that clinical educators have for their students, listed in Table 3.2. We would suggest that other characteristics are those associated with adult learners. McAllister (1997) discussed these more fully. In brief, according to Knowles (1980) and Brookfield (1986), adult learners are characterized by:

- becoming more self-directing, although they may chose dependence on the teacher in some circumstances
- seeking autonomy in learning
- using their life experiences as a rich resource for learning
- learning better through experiential means
- linking learning needs to life circumstances at the time, e.g. the need to acquire job-related skills
- being more problem centred for immediate performance in life circumstances.

Students are encouraged to evaluate themselves against these criteria, and those expectations in Table 3.2, and to determine areas of strength and areas for development.

Learning exercise 3.4: evaluation of self as an effective adult learner.

- How would you rate yourself against these characteristics and expectations?
- Which ones do you possess/can you fulfil already?
- Which ones do you emphasize?
- Which ones might you need to develop?

The clinic is an ideal setting for the development of adult learning approaches because the needs of clients provide real problems requiring an immediacy of response, and the imperative to develop job-related clinical skills motivates students to take responsibility for their learning. Working with clients also requires students to apply deep learning approaches (Marton and Saljo, 1984), i.e. they need to engage fully with the learning task, see the whole picture or whole person, draw on their propositional as well as their personal practical knowledge and emerging professional craft knowledge, and actively search for meaning in the wealth of clinical information at hand. This can be challenging for students who have 'got by' in theory subjects with surface learning approaches, which use rote learning, and are characterized by low motivation and only sufficient engagement with the learning task to pass. Clinical education requires high levels of internally derived motivation, effort and a commitment to doing more than just enough to pass – doing all that can be done to provide the best client care.

Good communication and interpersonal skills

Although students value effective teaching behaviours as outlined above, research consistently identifies that students rate more highly, or mention as important more frequently, the communication and interpersonal attributes and characteristics of their clinical educators (Emery, 1984; Cupit, 1988; Jarski et al., 1990; Neville and French, 1991; Onuoha, 1994; Williams and Webb, 1994; Paukert and Richards, 2000; Shanfield et al., 2001). Table 3.4 lists some of these interpersonal and communication attributes and characteristics.

We know less of the interpersonal and communication characteristics and skills expected by clinical educators of students, although the list of expectations compiled by Alsop and Ryan (1996) (see Table 3.2) suggests several valued interpersonal attributes. These would include those listed in Table 3.5. We have added others that we value in our students. What other communication skills and interpersonal attributes do you as students or clinical educators value in students?

Table 3.4 Interpersonal and communication attributes of clinical educators valued by students

- Friendly
- Helpful
- Forthcoming with information
- Approachable
- Awareness of student as a person and future colleague
- Being inspirational and enthusiastic
- Being encouraging and emotionally supportive
- Rapport and respect
- Listening and answering
- Asking questions appropriately

Based on Cupit (1988), Irby (1986), Neville and French (1991)

Table 3.5 Interpersonal and communication attributes of students valued by clinical educators

- Well prepared, organized, punctual
- Friendly, but not inappropriately so
- Presents professionally
- Helpful
- Forthcoming
- Reliable
- Responsible
- Enthusiastic
- Respectful
- Ethical
- Sensitive to the needs of others (clients, peers, clinical educator)
- Listens
- Responsive
- Asks appropriate questions

The lists of desirable interpersonal and communication skills and attributes for clinical educators and students look remarkably similar. These attributes and skills need attention and development for learning relationships to grow and be effective. Students and clinical educators can work as partners in the learning relationship to support this development. Development of personal skills will be discussed in more detail in Chapter 4.

A framework for considering learning relationships

The desirable attributes of clinical educators listed in Table 3.4 were affirmed in a study of the experience of being a clinical educator (McAllister, 2001), which highlighted the primacy of interpersonal skills in being an effective clinical educator. That study revealed four elements in clinical educators' experiences of being in relationship with others, particularly with their students. These are listed in Table 3.6, together with aspects that make up those elements. Although these were derived from the experiences of clinical educators, they also represent values and attributes sought in students (Alsop and Ryan, 1996; Lincoln et al., 1997a). We would suggest that they could form a parallel set of characteristics that facilitate learning relationships between students and their clinical educators, and we discuss them in this way, drawing on examples from the work of McAllister (2001) and a study of students experiencing difficulties in clinic (Nemeth, 2004).

Table 3.6 Elements of the dimension 'A sense of relationship with others'

Being people oriented

Perceiving others:
    as having individual styles and needs
    as worthy of dignity and respect
    as growing, changing individuals

Values in relating to others:
    authenticity, trust, empathy and sensitivity, empowerment and mutuality
    openness about humanness and fallibility
    caring

Seeking to implement values and perceptions in relating to others:
    developing good communication
    responding to students' emotional as well as learning needs
    putting in extra time and effort

From McAllister (2001)

Being people oriented

Being people oriented in the clinical education context means 'giving priority to people in the day-to-day flow of the workplace. It involves being alert to people's emotional states, needs and values, and seeking to meet these needs in a way that is congruent with personal values' (McAllister, 2001). In people-oriented clinical educators, the nurturing and management of relationships is important as a way of achieving desired goals and outcomes, but does not preclude a dual focus on tasks when required. People-oriented clinical educators 'desire to relate well to people' and seem to have 'a knack for finding and bringing out the best in people'.

As clinical educators, we expect that our students will also be people oriented, and to move from being self-focused to adoption of client-centred approaches to therapy (Lincoln et al., 1997a). Nemeth (2004), in her investigations of students' experiences on placements, has found that students who succeed in clinical placements, especially those working with 'difficult' clinical educators, are not only client focused but also quite clinical educator focused. Clinical educators perceived as 'difficult' by students include those with unrealistic expectations, poor interpersonal skills, poor time management and organization, or those who are unduly critical and offer little or no positive reinforcement. Students adopt a range of strategies for successfully managing such clinical educators. These are discussed further in Chapter 4.

Perceiving others

Perceiving others in the clinical education context means having a desire and ability to see people as they really are, not how we might wish them to be. It means being alert to others' learning styles and needs and interests, emotions, desires and aspirations. This ability to perceive others in this way is a fundamental attribute of health professionals that allows them to deliver ethical, client-centred care (Corey et al., 1998). It is an ability that we actively seek to socialize and foster in our students with regard to their clients.

Clinical educators are exhorted (see, for example, Lincoln et al., 1995) to be alert to and adapt to their students' learning styles. Discussion of students' learning styles and learning needs is suggested as a routine part of the orientation phase of students' placements (Romanini and Higgs, 1991). Conversely, however, little emphasis is given in preparing students for clinical placements to recognize the individual styles and needs of their clinical educators. However, as Nemeth (2004) has discovered, students who read the particularities and peculiarities of their clinical educators are effectively better able to manage their clinical placements, even when they are not doing well (see Vignette 3.2).

In addition, clinical educators are not encouraged to discuss their needs and aspirations for placements and for professional growth with their students. We would suggest that this results partly from a lack of recognition that clinical education can be a place for learning together. Also, some clinical educators have a belief that they should be able to answer all their students' questions and fear that to disclose their professional learning needs might make them vulnerable to students

> ## Vignette 3.2: example of a student who 'manages' her clinical educator
>
> It seemed to me that my clinical educator believed that the only correct view on any client management issue was her view. Early on in the placement I tried to present some alternative views based on the more current theory I had access to at university. She became really defensive when I did this. I knew I wouldn't be able to have a discussion with her about her defensiveness so from then on I tried to avoid any discussions that would potentially create conflict between us, unless of course client care was going to be compromised. I just figured that to maintain a harmonious relationship with her I needed to submerge some of my personality and opinions and that was OK, I still learned a tremendous amount because she was very skilful. I think if I had been perceived as a threat by her she wouldn't have allowed me all the opportunities I had to watch her at work.

(McAllister, 2001). Approaching clinical placements as an opportunity for mutual learning and growth and role-modelling of life-long learning might address such concerns.

Perceiving others as worthy of dignity and respect are fundamental ethical principles of health professionals (Corey et al., 1998), and the recognition of the capacity for all individuals to grow and change is a fundamental tenet of humanistic approaches to psychology, education and therapy (Maslow, 1968; Rogers, 1969a; Egan, 1990). Anderson (1988) highlighted that growth and change for both students and clinical educators are two outcomes of successful supervision. Clinical educators need to have faith and optimism that their students have the potential for change and growth, and be able to accord them dignity and respect, even when things are not going well in a placement. Similarly, students need to find a way to respect the contribution that their clinical educators can make to their growth, even when educators are giving them negative feedback or intend to fail them on the placement. Mutual respect can be maintained more readily if fundamental values in relating to each other are held and enacted.

Values in relating to others

Clinical educators value and demonstrate a range of values in relating to others (McAllister, 2001). These include authenticity, trust, empathy, sensitivity, empowerment, mutuality, openness about one's humanness and fallibility, and caring. Mutuality is the close working together of an educator and learner, and is a crucial condition for adult learning, an approach that we have previously mentioned as an appropriate foundation for clinical education. Others are characteristic of humanistic educators (Rogers, 1967). Some of these values underpin the codes of ethics of health professionals, and are values we discuss, assess, role-model and socialize into our students.

In a study of classroom teachers who enjoyed their work, Nias (1989) found major themes of 'being yourself' and 'being whole'. McAllister (2001) also found a theme in clinical educators of 'being real': participants enjoyed their role as clinical educators when they could be authentically themselves with their students. Acknowledgment of one's humanness and fallibility were values found in the more experienced clinical educators. They had passed through the 'survival stage' of becoming a clinical educator where the need to establish control and credibility makes openness too risky, and potentially damaging to one's emerging identity as an educator. Our experience with students over the years leads us to suggest that the same applies to students. We do know from the work of Chan et al. (1994) that students regard openness as something to be avoided for fear of exposing their weaknesses to clinical educators, which might make them more vulnerable in the assessment process.

Learning exercise 3.5: self-assessment task for students and clinical educators

Circle the values that you believe you demonstrate in your relationships with educators and learners, and add others that are important to you.

authenticity   mutuality   sensitivity

     empathy   openness

     empowerment   caring

trust   self-acceptance

Seeking to implement values and perceptions in relating to others

Clinical educators who successfully develop and maintain learning relationships with students do so by developing good communication, responding to students' emotional as well as learning needs, and putting in extra time and effort in their clinical educator role (McAllister, 2001). Students who develop and maintain learning relationships with their clinical educators use similar skills. Personal and communication skills used by clinical educators and students are discussed in more depth in Chapter 4.

Responding to the emotional needs of others takes not only skill, but also time. Successful learning outcomes for students require deep learning approaches (Marton and Saljo, 1984) and these also take time. Similarly, McAllister (2001) found that successful clinical educators were those willing to put in time and effort with their students. One spoke of this willingness thus:

> I could choose to not take the time but the students are people and I want to know them as people and that takes time . . . commitment and imparting a bit of yourself . . . I don't think I could slap 'em through . . . it would take a lot of the enjoyment out of it for me . . . it's well worth the investment of time.

This section has discussed four major aspects of effective learning relationships. Take some time now to self-assess on these aspects, and then reflect on the impact of these aspects of yourself on your learning relationships.

Learning exercise 3.6: self-assessment task – how would you rate yourself on the following elements of being in a learning relationship?

Scale: 1 always – 5 never
I am highly people oriented
I perceive others as having individual styles and needs
I perceive others as worthy of dignity and respect (no matter how challenging my relationship with them becomes)
I perceive others as growing, changing individuals (no matter how challenged they seem on occasions)
I respond to others' emotional needs
I am willing to put in extra time and effort to ensure learning occurs
I am a 'control freak'; I like things done 'my way'

Barriers to learning relationships and some approaches to managing problems in learning relationships

The previous section considered aspects that facilitate good learning relationships. Many things can go wrong in learning relationships. This section discusses some of the more common problems that can arise in the establishment and maintenance of learning relationships between clinical educators and students. These are listed in Table 3.7. This section also provides suggestions for management of these problems. The focus of this discussion is mainly on problems arising with clinical educators, because, as noted earlier, this is where most research has focused, and because it is clinical educators who bear the major responsibility for identifying and addressing problems in clinical education.

Table 3.7 Common barriers to establishing and maintaining learning relationships

Failure to balance task focus and people focus

Failure to perceive or respond to learning partners' individual styles and needs

Lack of attention to others' affective needs

Wanting to 'supervise' rather than 'educate'

Not seeing engagement in clinical education as a journey of growth and development

Failure to give appropriate and timely feedback

Protecting students from failure

Cultural differences

A clash of values

Putting in too little or too much time and effort

Not being authentically yourself

Failure to balance task focus and people focus

Becoming people oriented is a developmental process for both clinical educators (Christie et al., 1985; Brammer, 1996; McAllister, 2001) and students (Lincoln et al., 1997a). This process of personal development is discussed further in Chapter 4. A number of factors impede movement from being self-focused to people focused, including anxiety about a range of factors associated with students being on placement (Chan et al., 1994), and clinical educators' anxieties about being able 'to fit everything in' (McAllister, 2001), inability to manage dilemmas of time experienced by clinical educators (Edwards, 1996), and time management problems experienced by students (Lincoln et al., 2002). These factors are also explored further in Chapter 4.

Failure to perceive or respond to learning partners' individual styles and needs

Although we are encouraged to match our supervisory style to students' levels of competence (Anderson, 1988) and learner task maturity (Higgs, 1992), research consistently shows that clinical educators fail to do this (Anderson, 1988; Kenny, 1996; Joshi and McAllister, 1998). We tend to adopt or develop one supervisory style (often a dominant and controlling one) and to use this regardless of students' expressed needs and levels of competence. Not only does this frustrate the achievement of students' independence and learning goals, it also makes supervision more time-consuming and burdensome than it need be. Furthermore, it stifles the professional development of clinical educators, their ability to be flexible and innovative in supervision, and restricts their progress towards professional artistry.

Lack of attention to others' affective needs

As well as a failure to adapt to students' individual learning needs, research consistently shows that clinical educators do not pick up on or respond to students' emotions (Pickering, 1984; Anderson, 1988). Clinical educators often fail to identify the verbal and non-verbal cues from students that they are stressed, anxious, frightened, sad or traumatized or, if they do, they apparently choose to gloss over the situation (Kenny, 1996). The clinical environment is full of situations that challenge students' emotional equilibrium. Unless students' affective needs are attended to, learning may be impeded (Boud et al., 1985; Mandy, 1989). Clinical educators need to be more alert to students' needs, address those that are within their scope of responsibility, and know when to refer students for counselling.

Students are not in a position to be responsive to their clinical educators' affective needs. The power imbalance between clinical educators and students makes this difficult and, in addition, students and clinical educators need to avoid becoming enmeshed in 'games' (Berne, 1966) that might jeopardize assessor/student roles. However, they should be sensitive to the ebb and flow of time demands and pressures on their clinical educators, and avoid making undue or untimely demands on their clinical educators. Being responsive to their clinical educators' needs can be as simple as taking as much responsibility as appropriate for finding out information (rather than always having to ask the clinical educator), being punctual and organized with paperwork, choosing a time of day suitable to the clinical educator to raise concerns, and providing positive feedback to the clinical educator.

Wanting to 'supervise' rather than 'educate'

If the volume and nature of feedback received at universities from clinical educators in the field are reliable indicators, it could be assumed that many clinical educators would rather students came 'clinic ready', with pre-packaged, clinically ready knowledge and skills. This would allow clinical educators to function merely as supervisors so that all that was required was to provide supervised opportunities for students to apply and practise already developed knowledge and skills, rather than have to facilitate students' learning of clinically relevant knowledge (see McAllister, 1997, for a discussion of the distinctions between supervision and education). However, helping students access their propositional knowledge and transform this into professional craft knowledge is an important role for clinical educators.

Similarly, students complain that clinical educators do not know what they are doing as supervisors and do not know everything as clinicians. Viewing their learning relationship as one of mutual growth and development might enable both parties to find the process of clinical education more productive and satisfying.

Not seeing engagement in clinical education as a journey of growth and development

Some clinical educators assess students early in placements as not being competent. They might have expected students to come 'clinic ready' and might judge those students who are not 'clinic ready' as being 'not very good students'. They do not, as described by one clinical educator in the study by McAllister (2001), remain 'always optimistic for the potential for growth and change'. Similarly, some students are very critical of the personal and professional failings of their clinical educators. Both parties need to be prepared for and supported during clinical placements to recognize the parallel journeys of professional and personal growth that students and their clinical educators are on. This might reduce the attrition of novice clinical educators who face challenges early on in their careers as educators, and never take students again. It might also reduce the unrealistic and unfair expectations placed on students by some clinical educators. Appropriate communication and feedback would make for a more supported and enjoyable journey for both parties.

Failure to give appropriate and timely feedback

For a profession engaged in the business of communication, it is surprising that in speech–language pathology clinical education, one of the biggest, recurrent problems is lack of feedback – from clinical educators to students (Anderson, 1988; Best and Rose, 1996) and from students to clinical educators. One reason that students fail to provide feedback to their clinical educators is fear of adverse assessment (Chan et al., 1994). These issues are explored further in Chapters 6 and 7. One reason that clinical educators fail to provide timely feedback to students may be their 'fear of failing them' and their desire to 'protect themselves and protect students' from the consequences of failure (McAllister, 2001).

Protecting students from failure

Clinical educators have responsibilities to the universities that place students with them, their clients and their professional bodies, and to the students themselves to fail students who are not yet competent and safe to practise. Adopting a humanistic view of the educator's role (Rogers, 1967) and respecting the capacity of individuals to grow and change might not be enough to prevent students' failure on placement. However, by supporting students through failure with clear and fair assessments of their skills and deficits, and helping to preserve their self-esteem and self-identity as growing, capable individuals, clinical educators can empower students to learn from the experience of failure. Students in Nemeth's study (2004) who received this respect and support talked of the experience as one of 'truly learning', and celebrated the personal and professional growth that they achieved by successfully managing their failure.

Cultural differences

The movement of peoples around the world and the consequent population diversity has had an enormous impact on the diversity of the health professions and student populations at universities (Pickering and McAllister, 1997). As a result, clinical educators and students from diverse cultural backgrounds will be interacting and learning with each other in clinical education contexts. How we perceive, think, talk and act are culturally determined (Hofstede, 1997). Unless both parties are prepared for cross-cultural interactions and communication, what should merely be 'difference' can become 'problematic'.

Students (and clinical educators) from minority cultures may experience, in the clinical setting, differences in approaches to teaching and learning, attitudes to health, wellness, disease and illness, personal and professional behaviours, and verbal and non-verbal communication. Students report discomfort with differences in communication style and content, and assertive behaviours expected in Western health and education settings (Stewart et al., 1996). If students are communicating in the clinical setting in a language other than their first language, processing time may be slower, because they may need to comprehend what has been said, translate it into their first language, prepare an answer and translate back. Clinical educators sometimes equate slow reaction time with lack of knowledge and skill (Stewart et al., 1996).

Clinical educators may also not pick up on subtleties of verbal and non-verbal communication with students, and misread students' responses and intents. They may make untimely or inappropriate comments or feedback. Clinical educators are often unduly critical of students' written language skills (Stewart et al., 1996), showing little understanding of English as an international language (Crystal, 1997) and of what it means to live in a multicultural society. Students faced with these cross-cultural communication breakdowns and inappropriate assessments of their competence sometimes feel that they are the victims of racism (Stewart et al., 1996). The converse, of course, can also apply – that students hold culturally determined expectations of interactions and clinical educators from cultures other than their own.

One way of avoiding such problems is for students and clinical educators to be better prepared for intercultural communication and cross-cultural interactions. Pickering and McAllister (2000) discuss principles of these and their applications to practice. The observance of good communication practices, considered in Chapter 4, would also help avoid culturally based miscommunications.

A clash of values

Sometimes, what looks like a clash of values is in fact differing amounts of attention paid to aspects of one's role, e.g. clinical educators have been heard to lament that their students are not sensitive, caring and compassionate towards clients' needs. Students, in turn, may complain bitterly once back at university on completion of placements that their clinical educators did not 'care about them as people' and had unrealistic expectations of them. In fact, the opposite may be the truth. Students new to a clinical setting might respond to the situation by being task focused and self-focused, appearing to be insensitive to client needs, but are in fact unable to tune into much more than their own survival needs. Apparently unreasonable and uncaring clinical educators might in fact be asserting control over students to complete vital paperwork related to clients in order to ensure that legal, ethical and client care needs are met as first priority, with student needs coming second to those. Edwards (1996) discussed this tension as resulting from the dilemma of purpose, acknowledging that clinical educators must function as both clinicians and educators. Certainly, there are clinical educators who have succumbed to managerialist and economic rationalist workplace pressures and value 'the bottom line' more than relationships, and students whose priorities are elsewhere than their studies (McInnis et al., 2000). However, most students and clinical educators enter and stay in health professions because they have a core set of humanistic values. Further, cultural differences might create differing perspectives on ways of viewing situations and interacting with individuals. Where a clash of values seems apparent, intercultural practice principles (Yoshikawa, 1987) can be adopted, and dialogue entered into, to find common ground, to affirm the centrality of client care and treating others well.

Putting in too much or too little time and effort

Students or clinical educators rarely put in too little time to clinical education. Sometimes students cannot balance the pressure of university subjects with clinical placements (Chan et al., 1994), and both of these with work and personal commitments (McInnis et al., 2000). Sometimes students may appear to do too little because they have not been clearly briefed about the expectations of them (Goodfellow et al., 2001). Clinical educators in managerialist workplaces may occasionally focus more on other roles and neglect the learning relationship. Often, the reverse becomes problematic. Some clinical educators invest too much of themselves and their time into students and clinical placements, and fail to balance these with the rest of their work roles, and with the rest of their lives. Alternatively, they may have a rapid turnover of students or a run of students with problems. As a result, burnout is a problem for clinical educators (Ray, 1984; McAllister, 2001). When the dilemmas of time and purpose noted by Edwards (1996) are not effectively managed, clinical educators need to critically self-appraise the way that they structure and manage student placements and their learning relationships.

Students experience fatigue and stress (Alsop and Ryan, 1996; Nemeth, 2004), and they often express anxiety about the workload expected of them on placements and complain of the amount of after-hours' time required (Chan et al., 1994). Some students may also experience burnout; these may be the students who become repeatedly ill, take time out of the course or leave the course before they complete their degree. All parties involved in clinical education need to be alert to the possibility of burnout in students and take preventive action. Although anxiety about a new experience is normal and clinical placements do require time and effort, clinical educators need to be realistic in their expectations of their students, and students need to have clear guidelines and be empowered to be assertive if expectations are unrealistic.

Not being authentically yourself

Students and their clinical educators often feel under pressure to be the 'perfect student' or the 'perfect clinical educator'. Students report feeling pressured to be like their clinical educators (Chan et al, 1994; Nemeth,

2004), who in turn may feel that they are expected by students to behave like 'the perfect speech language pathologist' and to 'know everything' (McAllister, 2001). Clinical educators who are mature personally and professionally give themselves permission to make mistakes, and to be their own person (McAllister, 2001). They also give their students permission to be authentically themselves and the room to develop their own professional personas. One clinical educator in the study by McAllister (2001) spoke of how she would tell her students:

> I don't want clones of myself; you need to be yourselves. If you're not, it's phoney and you can pick that, and it's tiring for you.

Students may find it hard to be authentically themselves, because they fear negative assessments by their clinical educators (Chan et al., 1994; Nemeth, 2004), a topic that is explored further in Chapter 7. Learning to be authentically yourself is one of the goals of personal development discussed in Chapter 4.

Conclusion

The clinical education context offers many opportunities for clinical educators and students to learn together. Personal and interpersonal skills are critical to fostering an environment where mutual learning can occur. The development of these skills is an ongoing task for students and clinical educators which is considered in the next chapter.

Development of personal skills

As noted in Chapter 3, clinical education is essentially a person-focused process. Pickering (1987) proposed that clinical education is concerned with human growth and change for the client, the student and the supervisor. Supervision asks students to 'merge who they are personally with whom they are becoming professionally' (Pickering, 1987, pp. 108–109), and compels clinical educators and students to examine a range of aspects of themselves. This chapter considers personal skills that contribute to successful learning relationships between clinical educators and students. Four areas of personal skills are considered: a sense of self; interpersonal communication skills; self-management; and management of others' emotions, time and tasks. Strategies that can be used to promote personal skill development are considered. The chapter begins with a series of vignettes that illustrate stages of development of personal skills in clinical educators and students.

Stages of development in being a clinical educator

Becoming a clinical educator is inherently a process of growth and development (Christie et al., 1985; Brammer, 1996; Edwards, 1996; McAllister, 2001). There are some similarities in this process with those described for classroom teachers (Katz, 1972; Glickman, 1980). These studies will be used to discuss Vignettes 4.1–4.5 provided below which describe growth and development in five clinical educators who participated in a study with McAllister (2001). The concepts of development from novice to expert (Benner, 1984) and of professional artistry (Fish and Twinn, 1997; Fish and Coles, 1998) have been used to describe stages in this developmental process. In addition, the experience of burnout is also illustrated. As you read these vignettes illustrating personal growth, and burnout, consider which clinical educator you might identify with.

The novice clinical educator

Vignette 4.1: Jenny – a novice clinical educator

Jenny was a relatively new graduate when the local university speech–language pathology programme, which was short of placements, rang and coerced her to take a student. She did not feel ready to take on a student, because she did not yet feel clinically competent. She described how 'it is hard enough to think what to do yourself without having to explain it to someone else'. She was concerned about what she could tell students and talked of a 'fear of their knowledge', that 'students might know more than I do'. She also dreaded being watched and admitted she was very anxious about managing a caseload and a student – how would she 'fit it all in'? However, she could see that having to do so might be good for her learning. She also thought that, because she was close to her own student experiences, she 'might be able to be understand what the student was going through' and help them become comfortable in the setting. Nevertheless, Jenny agreed to take a student, and 'just get in and do it, don't think too much about it'. She decided to manage by being 'extremely organized, putting on a calm front and acting competent'. As she had no strategies for juggling client load and student clinical education load, she found she had to work long hours to fit everything in, placing herself at risk of fatigue and burnout. Jenny did not seek professional development in her new role of clinical educator, instead drawing on images of her own 'best-ever clinical educator' as a role-model. Initially she took few opportunities to reflect on what she was doing, although she did gradually draw on support from colleagues.

Jenny illustrates the self-focus of the 'survival stage' described in novice schoolteachers and clinical educators by Katz (1972) and Christie et al. (1985). As with the novice clinical educators described by Christie et al. (1985) and Edwards (1996), Jenny saw her role as passing on content, and as a result experienced anxiety about her knowledge base. She felt a high need for control. She struggled with the dilemma of time described by Edwards (1996); she always felt time pressured. However, Jenny quickly managed to rise above her self-focus to accommodate the needs of her student. She also engaged in inauthentic behaviour in putting on a calm front, rather than seeking to develop an authentic learning relationship, as described in Chapter 3, where both parties can be open about their vulnerabilities and learning needs. Jenny avoided reflection on how she was developing as a clinical educator, denying herself a valuable opportunity to learn from experience through reflection (Boud et al., 1985). However, when she began to seek discussion with her colleagues about her student, she was on her way to moving from novice to advanced beginner clinical educator status.

Moving from novice to advanced beginner clinical educator

Vignette 4.2: Emma – an advanced beginner clinical educator

Emma had been working as a speech–language pathologist for a couple of years, and was taking students for the second semester in a row at the time of her participation in the study. She described herself as 'someone with a passion for learning', who wanted to be a 'helper' to her students in their learning and growth. She acknowledged that she had 'a need to be liked' by her students and 'wanted to be sensitive to her students' and responsive to their needs. However, she liked to be well organized and 'for things to be in control'. Emma was highly reflective and conceptualized and discussed her experiences of becoming a clinical educator using the metaphor of 'getting comfortable in new shoes'. With some students, the new shoes were easy to wear, but, with others, she was under considerable pressure and the new shoes gave her 'blisters'.

In some of these challenging interactions, Emma felt 'out of control', something she did not like. After evaluating progress in client care and student learning at the mid-placement assessment, Emma realized she would need to change her style with some students. It hurt her to have to take on a role with some students that required her to appear insensitive to their needs as she attempted to extricate herself from unproductive ways of interacting, and pushed students to place client care above their own needs. However, she knew that to protect client care and ensure student growth, she would have to manage students differently.

She realized that she was not solely responsible for whether students passed or failed their placements, and began to insist that they took some initiative for making the changes required to meet placement and client goals. In becoming more assertive and confrontational with some students, she found it extremely challenging to 'risk not being liked and to live with feeling like she didn't know where things were going'.

Emma possessed many of the characteristics of humanistic educators described by Rogers (1967). She was sensitive to the needs of others, and wished to develop empowering relationships with her students. Emma was highly self-aware, something recommended as a key to success in being a clinical educator in Chapter 1. She was other focused rather than self-focused, but aware of her discomfort around issues of time management, control and being liked. Like most clinical educators, she struggled with Edwards' (1996) dilemmas of time, purpose and control: there was not enough time for all the tasks requiring her attention; she found it hard to juggle her dual responsibility for both clients and students; and she found it challenging to balance exerting control over students to ensure client care against allowing them freedom to learn and grow. However, she was able to reflect on these dilemmas in order to find more effective ways of managing them. Unlike new clinical educators described by Brammer (1996), Emma did not find assessment of students difficult, but instead was able to use it to redirect things for herself and her students. Like those clinical educators described by Christie et al. (1985), with some experience of the clinical education process, Emma had realized that she was not totally responsible for the success or failure of placements and that students also have a responsibility for learning. Recognition of individual students' learning needs led her to modifications of the placement programme and the development of more individualized learning programmes. She actively sought support and feedback from other clinical educators in her workplace, something that affirmed her reflection and helped her on her journey to developing competence as a clinical educator.

Developing competence in the role of clinical educator

Vignette 4.3: Robyn – a competent clinical educator

Robyn was a highly experienced clinician and clinical educator, working in a community setting with clients with complex needs. She had been taking students on placement for about 30 years, and found it very rewarding because it allowed her to 'put another hat on' (i.e. to have diversity in her work roles) and 'pass on her passion' for working with people with disabilities. Over many student placements Robyn had developed 'a plan', a general approach to conducting and managing placements. She felt that, because of the complexity of her clients' needs, 'students should fit in with the plan'. However, by what she called 'finding the best in people', she gave them room for creativity and individuality in their work with clients, once she was sure that they were 'putting clients first'. Robyn appeared unharried by time pressures, and liked to use what she referred to as 'chatting' to build and maintain learning relationships, check on how things were going from the perspective of clients, students and other staff, and to lead and educate the students. She also 'looked for the flow' in students' work with clients, as a further indicator that all was going smoothly. She was careful to 'nurture and support the students, rather than push them into anything'. Robyn was quite content with her 'plan' and not particularly willing to engage in reflection about her experiences as a clinical educator.

Robyn was a skilled clinical educator. She had a strong sense of herself as a person and of the values that mattered to her. She was highly other focused. She used chatting to build, maintain and monitor learning relationships, and demonstrated excellent communication skills. She possessed all the attributes valued by students in their clinical educators, as described in Chapter 3. She appeared not to experience dilemmas of time (Edwards, 1996), always having time to chat; however, she used such chatting efficiently for many purposes.

Robyn avoided dilemmas of purpose and control (Edwards, 1996) by insisting that students always put clients first and follow 'the plan'. She had found a way to balance people focus with task focus, by having a plan for organizing and structuring placements that gave students clear goals and messages, while at the same time seeking to nurture and support the students. She exerted a fair degree of control over placements and was unwilling to take risks and experiment with different ways of managing placements. She was also unwilling to openly critique her approach to clinical education. As a result, although competent in her clinical educator role, she was not seeking to extend her skills and pursue professional artistry as a clinical educator.

Pursuing professional artistry as a clinical educator

Vignette 4.4: Ann – pursuing professional artistry as a clinical educator

Ann had been working for several years as a speech–language pathologist and had been working full time as a student supervisor for 18 months when she participated in the study. She had a strong sense of herself as a clinician and educator, believing that 'the most important thing you bring into your job is yourself'. She had grown through the experience of being a clinical educator, through eliciting and acting upon feedback. She was now able to be open with her students and colleagues about her strengths and weaknesses. She held strong values about being an educator, and spoke of 'caring for' and 'respecting' students, and wanting them to be 'genuinely themselves as clinicians, not clones of [me]'. She saw her 'whole approach to life as being a collaborator', at home and at work, where she sought to collaborate with students to develop their placements to meet their own needs as well as those of their clients. In meeting students' needs, Ann placed enormous emphasis on 'talking things through and working things through' with them. She told how she had started off as a more structured and structuring clinical educator, but had learned over time how 'to be flexible' and 'scaffold student learning', by providing preparatory learning experiences so that students could safely engage with clients with reduced stress. She also was able to 'sit quietly', allowing students to direct the flow of conversation and the pace of their own learning, with what she called 'one ear listening', waiting for the right moment to provide input. Ann was not particularly susceptible to time pressures in the clinic, stating that 'things would take as long as they took'. This response to time meant that she worked long hours and became fatigued, something she realized she would need to address. She took great delight in reflecting on her growth and development as a clinical educator and in seeing her 'personal and professional boundaries blur', i.e. experiencing a sense of authenticity and wholeness.

Ann demonstrated many of the attributes of quality supervisors described by Fish and Twinn (1997). She had a principled approach to practice that she was able to articulate and which she exposed to critique. She was reflective and self-critical, and strove for growth and change. She valued the role of theory in her work and endeavoured to help students discover and apply theory to their practice. She successfully blended the role of enabler of learning and personal growth with the role of supervisor. She was aware of the value base of her approach and the moral dimensions of practice and education, and sought to model and articulate these for her students. These characteristics are the attributes of professional artists in clinical education.

Ann also showed skilful management of dilemmas of purpose and control (Edwards, 1996) and an ability to balance people focus with task focus. She could deliberately heighten her awareness (Torbert, 1978) to home in on what was important at the time and respond to students' learning needs. She demonstrated the individualization of student learning programmes and flexibility noted by Christie et al. (1985) to be a product of experience and confidence in the role of clinical educator. Unlike many clinical educators described by Anderson (1988), Kenny (1996) and others, she paid particular attention to students' affective needs and actively sought to promote their growth as people as well as professionals. In developing a flexible scaffold for learning, one that could be individualized to students' and clients' needs, she had created what Higgs (1993) referred to as a liberating programme system, i.e. one that provides structure to support student learning (and in this case also protect clients), but which liberates students to learn in their preferred manner. She was a truly humanistic educator (Rogers, 1967) in values, process and desired goals. She was open, and actively sought to develop relationships with her students in which both parties could be authentically themselves, and learn and grow. Ann acknowledged to herself and her students that time management and personal organization were issues for her. She recognized that she needed to learn to manage these better in order to avoid burnout. Vignette 4.5 illustrates burnout in an experienced clinical educator. Not all clinical educators experience this, and we do not mean to suggest that it is a normal endpoint of the journey of professional growth and development for clinical educators.

Suffering burnout as a clinical educator

Vignette 4.5: Annette – suffering burnout as a clinical educator

Annette was an experienced speech–language pathologist and full-time clinical educator. She liked the fact that students 'kept her on her toes'. She felt it was 'important to know yourself' before becoming a clinical educator. In reflecting on her development as a clinical educator, Annette believed that time management was still a challenge for her, but that she had changed over the years as a clinical educator from 'being controlling' and 'taking too much responsibility' for students' passing or failing, to learning to 'step back' and allow students 'the freedom to learn from mistakes'. The university had sent Annette a series of failing students, because of her skills as a clinical educator, her capacity to be 'always optimistic for people's capacity for growth and change', and because she was nurturing and supportive. To ensure that client care was not compromised at the same time as being supportive to students, she worried that she was returning to her old style of controlling, rather than her preferred style of enabling. She tried indirectly to give the constructive feedback that might change student behaviour without 'bursting the bubble' of their fragile self-esteem, but found herself lost in long, convoluted, ineffectual conversations. She found herself 'lying awake at night worrying' about what she was doing with her students and what she described as her 'woolly thinking'. She became quite self-critical and doubted her competence. At the time of her participation in the study she was physically and emotionally exhausted, and felt 'quite depleted, that there was nothing left for me'. After much critical self-reflection, she left her full-time clinical educator position to return to clinical work.

Burnout has been described in individuals who work with people as a state characterized initially by emotional exhaustion, leading to depersonalization and reduced personal accomplishment (Maslach, 1982). Burnout is recognized as common in the health, human services and education sectors (Swidler and Ross, 1993; Lubinski, 1994). Annette was displaying several of the features of individuals with burnout as described by Maslach (1982) and Cherniss (1980). She was self-critical and had lost her sense of self-identity as an effective educator, and her sense of agency; she worried about taking action that she once would have taken with confidence. Burnout is multifactorial in nature, but major contributing factors are sustained emotional labour, constant change and time pressures, and inability to respond to the increasing complexities of the workplace. Emotional labour is a recognized risk factor associated with caring in the health professions (Staden, 1998). Annette's experience makes it clear that emotional labour applies in clinical education settings also. Emotional labour involves manipulating one's emotions in order to maintain a caring demeanour. A lack of authenticity in relationships, suppressed emotions, and incongruence between the sense of self and sense of being a carer/educator may result. Unlike some individuals experiencing burnout, Annette was aware of what was happening to her and was not engaged in depersonalizing. As a humanistic educator, Annette maintained her strong people focus and values of respect and sensitivity, caring and willingness to invest time and emotional energy in facilitating student growth. Other factors contributing to Annette's burnout appear to have been several years of rapid student turnover, known to be problematic for some clinical educators (Ray, 1984), over-investment of self, a stressful work environment, lack of support or leadership from her manager, and poor time management skills. Like many clinical educators who are not protected from burnout, Annette's skills as a clinical educator have been lost to the profession, because she has not returned to clinical education for many years now.

Vignettes 4.1–4.4 illustrate a continuum of development of personal skills as applied to being a clinical educator, whereas Vignette 4.5 illustrates burnout. Vignettes 4.1–4.4 show that one's sense of self grows in the role of clinical educator. Communication skills are refined. Skills in managing self and others in the clinical education context are developed with experience and support. Clinical educators come to their role with many personal skills in place which can be enhanced for the role;

students, however, often need to develop the basics of these skills and attributes, as can be seen in the vignettes in the next section.

Stages of development in being a student

There has been little longitudinal study of the development of allied health students as they progress through their professional preparation. However, reflection on our experience as clinical educators calls to mind clear images of students with whom we have worked. Below, we present three vignettes (4.6–4.8) of students who typify the novice, intermediate and competent entry level students with whom we have worked over the last 25 years.

The novice student clinician

Vignette 4.6: Carol – a novice student

Carol is in the second year of a 4-year undergraduate degree in speech–language pathology. This semester Carol is required to work on her own with a child. Previously she has worked with a child in the supportive context of a mentoring relationship with a more experienced student. Initially Carol is 'terrified' and 'extremely nervous'. Carol is able to identify that these feelings are related to fear of the unknown, especially about whether her client will like her and whether he will be compliant. Carol is also concerned about talking with the client's parent and is worried that the parent will not have confidence in her skills. Each session with the client seems to 'fly by in no time' and Carol feels exhausted at the end of the session but is unsure why. Carol thinks a lot about her performance between sessions and sets goals such as 'talking to the parent more, giving clearer instructions to the client and presenting more confidently'. Carol is happy with her clinical educator who is friendly and approachable, although Carol wishes she would give her more direct answers to her questions and more written feedback after each session. She knows that her clinical educator watches each session and will 'bail her out' if things don't go well. Carol plans the management of her client from week to week and is focused on 'surviving' each session.

Novice student clinicians such as Carol bear a striking resemblance to professionals in the 'survival' stage, described by Katz (1972). They are highly anxious, underconfident and quite self-focused because they pay attention to the separate pieces of information, facts and features rather than being able to see the whole picture. They lack confidence in interactions with clients and their families, and have difficulty directing the behaviour of clients in therapy sessions. They have great difficulty applying clinical reasoning and making decisions. Novice student clinicians can be disorganized or rigidly over-organized, and they are typically poor time managers. Students in the total novice, survival stage need a high level of direction and structure to complete tasks and assistance to manage their anxiety. Tasks need to be simplified and timelines clearly laid out for them. Mawdsley and Scudder (1989) (see Chapter 1) describe this as using a 'telling' style of supervision. Novices require clear criteria for performance and prompt, explicit feedback on performance. They require good role-models of interpersonal communication skills, frameworks for applying theory to practice and generating clinically applicable (professional craft) knowledge, and modelling and explication of clinical reasoning and decision-making (McAllister and Rose, 2000). Through the use of scaffolded learning (see Vignette 4.4) novices can be supported to move to the intermediate stage, where they can consider broader views, values and attitudes, relate to their client as an individual, and begin to see 'the whole picture' (Alsop and Ryan, 1996).

The intermediate student

Vignette 4.7: John – the intermediate student

John is in his third year of a 4-year undergraduate degree in speech–language pathology. This semester his clinical educator has asked him to write a management plan for his client in lieu of detailed weekly session plans. This task is proving to be challenging for John because he must identify and prioritize all the goals for his client and think in both the long and short term, as well as beyond the clinical setting. John decides to conduct a school visit to help him achieve a more holistic view of the client. John feels both 'excited' and 'apprehensive' about talking to the client's teacher. He is particularly worried about the teacher asking him questions that he can't answer.

John has managed to establish a productive working relationship with his client's parents and he feels affirmed by the trust and respect that they communicate to him. In particular John and the parents are working together to keep the client motivated to participate in therapy. John is challenged to find the right level of difficulty for his treatment activities and also strives each week to make the activities fun and interesting for the client. He has found that he shares a common interest in football with his client so he successfully uses this to develop rapport and to design interesting activities. He is also experimenting with his interpersonal style with the client and he discovers that a 'high energy' style of interaction improves the response rate of the client and his level of enjoyment.

John illustrates how, as anxiety decreases and basic skill levels increase, students can become less self-focused and more other focused. They begin to focus on relationship building and maintenance with their clients, attend to more information at once, develop their knowledge and skills, and apply this to clinical reasoning. They develop beyond the immediate 'what needs to happen next' view to consider short-term goals for clients and themselves.

With this stage in place, students can begin to develop the panoply of knowledge, skills and attributes that characterizes competent professional practice. As for teachers in the consolidating stage (Katz, 1972), students can focus more on their clients (while beginning to be self-aware and reflective), and can take longer-term, truly holistic views of their clients, leading to improved planning and delivery of intervention. They can begin to develop flexibility, creativity and individuality in their work as clinicians. Their skills in communicating confidently and effectively with clients and clinical educators improve, and they can more effectively manage clients, as well as their clinical educators. They can competently follow routines and procedures, while knowing how to prioritize (Alsop and Ryan, 1996). Time management also improves. Students at the intermediate stage may still lack self-confidence and a sense of self as a clinician. As a result, a 'selling' style of supervision, as described by Mawdsley and Scudder (1989), may be appropriate. Such a style builds confidence as well as promoting competence, allowing growth towards entry level, new graduate status.

Competent, entry level student

Vignette 4.8: Sue – a competent, entry level student

Sue is completing her final placement before receiving her Masters in Speech–Language Pathology. Sue is excited about participating in this placement because for the first time she is feeling confident and in control of her clinical education experience. This placement will also allow her to work as part of a multidisciplinary team and she hopes that this will help her refine her interpersonal skills and further develop her professional identity as a speech–language pathologist. She looks forward to the weekly team meetings because the other team members direct questions and comments about her clients directly to her, and some of them have commented that they often forget that she is a student. Her clinical educator is happy to act in a collegial way with her and makes herself available to watch or discuss any aspects of client care that Sue is finding problematic. Sue is also enjoying participating fully in the speech and language pathology department's activities, e.g.

she has participated in a quality improvement project and a yearly planning meeting, and has been rostered to answer the phones during intake time. She has even helped her clinical educator out by standing in for her at a meeting when she was feeling unwell. Sue is enjoying working with her caseload and is 'pleased' and 'proud' that she can quickly develop a 'whole picture' of the client and the family, and implement 'truly functional and meaningful' treatment.

Sue shows development of a whole range of skills and attributes. She conducts herself professionally, and has developed a professional identity of her own. She is well organized, reliable and thorough. She manages her own time and workload well, and as a result has been given more responsibilities which she enjoys undertaking. She is a clear, assertive but sensitive communicator with all in the clinical context and feels comfortable to take on counselling roles with clients and families. She sees clients and their families as a whole and is able to use information from a range of contexts and people to reason her way from diagnosis to the development of appropriate treatment plans. Her clinical educator is able to use what Mawdsley and Scudder (1989) refer to as a delegating style of supervision, and to offer her many opportunities for extension of her skills beyond entry level.

    These three vignettes illustrate that both clinical educators and students go through stages of developing their self-knowledge, awareness, acceptance and identity, and their sense of self as a clinician/clinical educator. The nature of the development of personal skills is explored in the next section of this chapter. We consider four main areas of personal development as they relate to the clinical education context: a sense of self, specifically self-knowledge, self-awareness, self-acceptance and self-identity; interpersonal communication skills; self-management; and management of others. These areas pertain to dimensions 1, 2 and 4 of the model of the experience of being a clinical educator (McAllister, 2001) outlined in Chapter 1.

The development of personal skills

Readers will have deduced that, as authors and clinical educators ourselves, we highly value a humanistic approach to clinical work and education such as that described by Rogers (1961, 1962, 1967). Humanistic educators and clinicians possess a range of personal attributes such as sensitivity, empathy, caring, respect and mutuality. These attributes are predicated on a sense of self. A number of elements, as outlined in Chapter 1, make up one's sense of self. This section focuses only on self-knowledge and self-awareness, self-acceptance and self-identity.

Self-awareness and self-knowledge

Rogers (1961) wrote of self-awareness as meaning learning:

> . . . to become more adequate in listening to myself: so that I know, some-
> what more adequately than I used to, what I am feeling at any given
> moment – to be able to realise that I am angry, or that I do feel rejecting
> toward this person; or that I feel very full of warmth and affection for this
> individual; or that I am bored and uninterested in what is going on; or that
> I am eager to understand this individual or that I am anxious and fearful in
> my relationship with this person. All of these diverse attitudes are feelings
> which I think I can listen to in myself.
>
>   Cited in Kirschenbaum and Henderson (1990, p. 19)

Goleman (1995), in his discussion of emotional intelligence, considered self-awareness to be ongoing attention to one's internal states,
including both thought processes and moods or emotions. These are
sometimes referred to as metacognition and meta-mood. Developing
self-awareness and self-knowledge is viewed as essential for effective
work with clients, e.g. Egan (1990) states that 'it is essential to understand your own assumptions, beliefs, values, standards, skills, strengths,
weaknesses, idiosyncrasies, style of doing things . . . and the ways in
which these permeate your interactions with your clients' (pp. 24–25).
Lincoln et al. (1997a) suggested that this self-awareness needed for client
work is also desirable for understanding interactions between students
and clinical educators. Further, dialogue between clinical educators and
students can promote self-awareness in both parties (Goldhammer et al.,
1980; Johnston, 1994).

Self-acceptance and self-identity

Self-acceptance can be defined as acknowledging and valuing oneself,
with all one's strengths and limitations, identified and experienced as a
result of self-awareness and self-knowledge. Self-identity involves being
aware of the values, goals and abilities that are part of one's identities.
People actively seek to manage the impressions others have of them
(Goffman, 1959), a concept important to consider in students anxious to
be seen by clients and clinical educators as competent.

Self-acceptance does not imply complacency but rather understanding
and acknowledgement of one's real, authentic self. Self-acceptance also
does not preclude striving to bring one's current real self and one's future
ideal self (Markus and Nurius, 1986) closer together, and the use of strategies to manage impressions others have of us. However, as Rogers (1961)
noted 'I find I am more effective when I can listen acceptingly to myself
and be myself' (cited in Kirschenbaum and Henderson, 1990, p. 19). He

saw self-acceptance as essential for establishing conditions for interpersonal growth in clients and students, and for forming helping and learning relationships.

Self-acceptance was evident in the development of clinical educators and students illustrated in the vignettes. However, self-acceptance and the development of a reasonable and appropriate self-identity are often difficult for clinical educators and students to achieve. Many students start their professional education straight from high school and bring with them their ego-centrism and a host of other psychological and personality features, which characterize adolescence (Erickson, 1963). When confronted in the classroom with the need to work in groups and consider the needs of peers, and in the clinical setting with the needs and responsibilities for client care, many feel anxious and self-critical (Chan et al., 1994). Mature students may experience significant problems in adapting their existing self-identity as 'teacher' into that of 'therapist', or 'nurturing mother' into 'empowering professional'. Students may also come to the clinical setting with high expectations of themselves (Stengelhofen, 1993), often unrealistically reinforced by educators. Through the process of professional socialization (Cant and Higgs, 1999), students develop image(s) of their possible, future and ideal professional selves. These future selves may well be worthy and desirable in the long term, but not achievable in the short term, because personal and professional development needs to occur first.

Once students have developed an appropriate level of self-awareness, self-knowledge and self-acceptance, and have begun to develop personal and professional self-identities, they will be able to move from being self-focused to other focused. Similarly, once clinical educators have developed a sense of themselves as clinical educators, they move from a self-focus to being student centred and client centred.

Interpersonal communication skills

All professionals involved in the human service professions need good communication and interpersonal skills. These are founded on self-knowledge as discussed above, especially on our knowledge of our values and our preferred interaction style. What we value about others and ourselves will partially determine our interpersonal communications with others.

Values in interpersonal interaction

Table 3.5, in Chapter 3, listed a number of values that are important to clinical educators in learning relationships. We know much less about the values that students perceive to be important and how these change during the processes of personal maturation and professional socialization. Therefore this section discusses values known to be important to clinicians and educators, making reference to the development of these values when possible.

Trust

In discussing the importance of the interpersonal relationship in learning, Rogers (1967, cited in Kirschenbaum and Henderson, 1990) identified prizing, acceptance and trust as closely associated values, almost synonyms for each other. He described trust as 'a belief that the other person is somehow fundamentally trustworthy' (p. 309). This is what Annette meant in saying that she was 'always optimistic for people's capacity for growth and change' (see Vignette 4.5) – she trusted that they would achieve, given the right climate of trust and support. Similarly, Robyn (see Vignette 4.3) was talking about a fundamental level of trust in saying that she had could 'find the best in people'; she trusted that they would do their best by themselves, their clients and their colleagues.

Openness

Acknowledgement of our humanness and fallibility appears to be found only in more articulate and competent clinical educators (McAllister, 2001). Ann (see Vignette 4.4) and Annette (see Vignette 4.5) were happy to acknowledge their mistakes and encourage students to do the same, so that all could learn from them. Absence of overt acknowledgement of one's humanness and fallibility in new clinical educators is possibly the result of being in the 'survival stage' (Katz, 1972), where the need to establish control and credibility makes openness and acknowledgment of fallibility too risky. Similarly, students engaged in the double jeopardy of constructing a professional identity and passing assessment may feel that it is too risky to be open and acknowledge mistakes.

Caring

Caring, although somewhat unfashionable in the discourse of contemporary health professions according to Fish and Coles (1998), has important moral and philosophical bases (Noddings, 1984) that are worth noting. Caring, as discussed by Noddings, is embedded in relationships. Gilligan (1993) asserted that 'it is in their care and concern for others that women have both judged themselves and been judged' (p. 165). Certainly caring is a standard by which Emma, Robyn, Ann and Annette (see Vignettes 4.2–4.5) judge themselves as people and educators. The novice clinical educator Jenny (see Vignette 4.1), while demonstrating care for her clients and student, was unable to articulate this as an important value. As with novice clinical educators, students gradually come to embody caring as a value in their interactions with clients, as they make the move from self-focus to being other focused. Until students achieve this change of focus, they cannot deliver healthcare that is truly client centred, caring and sensitive to the needs of others.

Sensitivity and empathy

Sensitivity and empathy have also been emphasized as important values of humanistic educators. 'When the teacher has the ability to understand the student's reactions from the inside, has a sensitive awareness of the way the process of education and learning seems to the student, then again the likelihood of significant learning is increased' (Rogers, 1967, cited in Kirschenbaum and Henderson, 1990, p. 310). The same applies to students in their interactions with clients and peers. Goleman (1995) noted that 'empathy, another ability that builds on emotional self-awareness, is the fundamental "people skill"'.

As our values underpin our interpersonal communication style, clinical educators and students need to be encouraged to examine their values, beliefs and attitudes to a whole range of life dimensions and experiences. Pre-clinical preparation and discussions with clinical educators and peers on placements might explore, for example, values, beliefs and attitudes to communication and interaction styles, child-care practices, relationships, caring, wellness, illness, disability, death and dying, ethical dilemmas, people of different ages, gender, lifestyles, religion, language and culture. Professional development workshops or discussions with critical friends (Smith, 2001) or critical companions (Titchen, 1998) (see Chapter 6) can serve similar purposes of consciousness-raising for clinical educators. Both students and clinical educators need to be aware of their biases and prejudices, and the values and assumptions that underpin these. Legal and ethical requirements of practice also demand that students and their clinical educators understand their stages and styles of clinical, moral and ethical reasoning, how such reasoning may influence their decisions and interactions with clients, peers and educators, and how to evaluate and develop their reasoning. This topic is explored further in Chapter 5.

Communication skills

Good communication is particularly important in speech–language pathology, because it is both the process for goal attainment and the goal itself. The clinical education experience provides an opportunity for both students and clinical educators to discuss, analyse and practise communication skills.

As was noted in Chapter 3, interpersonal communication skills are consistently rated more highly by students than clinical educators' professional and teaching skills (Edwards, 1996; McAllister, 1997). Many of the skills valued by students relate to the use of empathic communication, as listed in Table 4.1.

Table 4.1 Skills associated with empathetic communication

Attending, acknowledging

Restating, paraphrasing

Reflecting

Interpreting

Summarizing, synthesizing

Supportive questioning

Giving feedback

Supporting (showing warmth and caring)

Checking perceptions

Being quiet

Adapted from Pickering (1987)

For students, learning to communicate effectively in a professional manner is a developmental process across the years of their professional preparation. As they move from a self-focus to an other focus, and take on more client management and counselling roles, they need to master a range of therapeutic and professional discourse types, and formal and informal styles associated with talking to children, parents, adult clients, other professionals, peers and their clinical educators. They need to master different genres associated with therapy sessions, presenting in case conferences, writing reports, file notes, etc. They need to learn to communicate in order to inform, cajole, influence, confront, control, instruct, support, empathize, counsel, receive, and respond to and provide feedback. They need to learn to use this range of communicative styles with clarity, compassion and assertion. They need to learn to do all this in a way that reflects their values and personality, i.e. 'their style'. As noted previously, emerging self-awareness, self-identity and self-confidence as a professional make the development of interpersonal communication skills a challenging task.

Students often find the development of assertive communication difficult. This may result partly from personality, but also from perceived power differences between themselves and clinical educators and other professionals. One student told us that she found her clinical educator to be:

> . . . very powerful, very assertive. I was the opposite. I found it very hard to deal with and it made me scared to go up to her and say 'look I'm having trouble yet again with this same thing. Can you help me?'

Students fear 'looking stupid' and also fear the impact that disclosure of lack of competence may have on their assessment by their clinical educator.

Another reason that students find assertive communication difficult with clients is recognition that they lack life experiences pertinent to the topic under discussion. Students tell us, for example, that:

> . . . it is hard to tell a mother how to fit in time for home practice when they know that you have no idea how busy a household with small children can be; and how can I tell this elderly gentleman to create opportunities for conversation when I know he is worried about what his friends think of him now.

Sometimes anxiety can make it hard for students to listen effectively and to 'hear' what has been said. They will often 'hear' the negative feedback but not the positive, or dwell unduly on critical comments. Clinical educators need to be sensitive to the possible negative impact of feedback on student anxiety and self-esteem, and take particular care to use 'accepting language' that conveys respect and optimism for student potential (Best and Rose, 1996). Look at the example in Table 4.2 of accepting and non-accepting language used in feedback to students and then work with Learning exercise 4.1 to practise constructing accepting language for use with students.

Table 4.2 Examples of accepting and non-accepting language used in feedback from clinical educators to student

---

Examples of accepting language used in feedback

It is often difficult to hold the attention of small children for longer than a few minutes. Perhaps next time you could try placing fewer objects on the table and see if this helps.

I got a sense that Mr X really didn't want to participate in the activity you gave him; I wonder what made you persist with trying to get him to do it?

Examples of non-accepting language used in feedback

Next time don't put so many objects out at once.

You missed Mr X's hints that he didn't want to do that activity; you need to get better at picking up non-verbal communication.

Learning exercise 4.1: using accepting language in feedback to students

Try rewriting this feedback in more accepting language

1. Your attempt at conducting the standardized test was unsuccessful.
2. You are boring this child!
3. Your interactional style with this gentleman was condescending.

As practising clinicians, clinical educators are assumed to have good communication skills. However, Pickering (1984), in a study of interpersonal communication between speech–language pathology clinical educators and students, found low levels of discourse features facilitative of good communication. These features included sharing aspects of one's humanness, being aware of the humanness of others, and discussions about supervisor–student interactions. Pickering found little discussion of feelings; students would share their feelings with their clinical educators but these would be responded to at a cognitive rather than an affective level. Furthermore, she found little evidence of mutual and collaborative decision-making. Kenny (1996) found similar patterns in her study of speech–language pathology clinical educators and students.

Many factors may contribute to these findings. Pickering (1984) questioned the perceptions held by clinical educators about their role and the goals of supervision. Additional factors are likely to be poor understanding of the role of reflection and exploration of feelings as a tool for learning (Boud et al., 1985), and poor management of dilemmas of time, purpose and control experienced by clinical educators (Edwards, 1996). Student factors also come into play. Students may be reticent to participate in dialogue, for a range of reasons. In addition, they often fail to request clarification or elaboration of clinical educators' comments (Anderson, 1988; Kenny, 1996).

The pursuit of clinical competence by students and of professional artistry by clinical educators calls for continual development of your communication skills and style. How would you self-evaluate your own communication strengths and weaknesses?

Learning exercise 4.2: self-assessment task

List features of your communication style that are your strengths and weaknesses. What is the impact of these features on establishing and maintaining learning relationships?

Strengths of my communication style:

Weaknesses of my communication style:

The impact of these strengths on learning and therapeutic relationships is:

The impact of these weaknesses on learning and therapeutic relationships is:

Developing communication skills

The development of communication skills requires active practice of skills, together with reflection on performance. Table 4.3 describes some strategies for improving communication skills in both students and clinical educators. Students' peers and clinical educators' critical friends can also provide feedback on their colleagues' communication.

Table 4.3 Ways of developing communication skills for students and clinical educators

Strategy	Prompts
Watching video recordings of interactions	Who is doing the least/most talking?
	How am I demonstrating that I'm listening to the other person?
	What does the other person's non-verbal behaviour tell me about how they are feeling?
	Did I respond to feelings appropriately?
	Did I seek clarification when I didn't understand?
	Did I feel comfortable with silences?
	Did the interaction fulfil my goals?
Direct feedback from students or clinical educators	Am I open to feedback about my communication skills?
	Are my strengths acknowledged?
	Are my weaknesses acknowledged?
Teaching through the supervisory relationship	Can I focus on the content as well as the process of communicating simultaneously?
	Do the same patterns of interactions occur with my clients and my students/clinical educator?
	Do I feel safe enough to give on-line feedback on communication skills during supervisory interactions?
Referral for communication skills training	Would I feel more comfortable practising my communication skills away from the clinical context initially?
Role-playing/simulations	Does rehearsal help prepare me for interactions?
	Can I take on roles?

Management of self and others

The management of oneself and of others can be seen to revolve around management of four key aspects: emotions (including anxiety), relationships, time and tasks. Both clinical educators and students need to learn to manage these aspects, in themselves and in others. The management of relationships is predicated on management of emotions, and on good interpersonal communication skills. The latter have already been discussed in the preceding section, and in Chapter 3. This section considers the management of emotions, time and tasks.

Managing emotions

Goleman (1995) suggests that 'the art of relationships is, in large part, skill in managing emotions in others' (Goleman, 1995, p. 43). Emotional intelligence involves the use of meta-mood monitoring and metacognition to sense and manage your own emotional state and needs, and those of others. For clinical educators, knowing yourself and using your emotional intelligence allows for identification and management of the affective aspects of being clinical educators.

Affective aspects of being a clinical educator

The affective aspects of being a clinical educator have received little attention in the clinical education literature. One study (McAllister, 2001) reported a range of emotions, tensions and dilemmas experienced in the various roles, tasks and relationships as described by five clinical educators. They talked of 'enjoying the job, enjoying working with the students, finding the funny side' of things, and of 'the joy of getting to know students'. Although they enjoyed their students, many experienced tiredness, fatigue, confusion (a sense of 'banging my head against the wall'), and a sense of 'being drained by students'. Emma, the advanced beginner described in Vignette 4.2 experienced 'an element of challenge, an element of frustration and annoyance, and an element of fear because I'm out of my depth'. Jenny, in Vignette 4.1, and Annette, in Vignette 4.5, talked of their 'anxiety' in having students.

Hargreaves and Tucker (1991) noted that guilt was a dominant emotion for teachers. They identified four 'guilt traps': a commitment to care, the open-endedness of teaching, accountability, and the persona of perfectionism. Unbounded, they can lead to emotional labour (Staden, 1998), and feelings of exhaustion and burnout, as was seen in Annette. The open-endedness of teaching is also experienced by clinical educators, as well as clinicians: 'there is never enough time to do everything that one wants to do'. Not only is 'the job never finished', but it is often 'not done well enough' according to the high standards set by health professionals for themselves. We also know from the work of Christie et al. (1985) and from Vignette 4.5 that many clinical educators feel overly accountable for students' success or failure on their clinical placements.

The experience of guilt can be further magnified when you are not managing the dilemmas of time, purpose and control described by Edwards (1996). It is important to note that, although the potential for dilemmas of purpose, time and control always exist in clinical education settings, such dilemmas need not necessarily eventuate. With experience and commonsense, dilemmas of purpose or control can be averted or managed by balancing and juggling priorities, and implementing a range of task and relationship management strategies. Being able to put things into perspective and manage the emotions of the job are personal skills that benefit from reflection and support.

Affective aspects of being a student

Clinical education generates many emotions in students, from joy in interactions with clients and families, and satisfaction derived from making a difference to people's lives, to anxiety and stress, to grief over the death of clients, to anger over negative feedback or evaluations received from clinical educators. As with clinical educators, there has been little investigation of emotions experienced by students arising from the clinical education context.

Students are increasingly committed to life roles other than those of a student and as a consequence may become disengaged from the student role and responsibilities (McInnis et al., 2001). They then may experience dilemmas of purpose on clinical placement. Although their primary purposes on clinical placement should be to provide the highest quality client care, and to learn, they might need to adopt a strategic task focus in order to juggle all their life roles, e.g. those of employee or parent. Students can also experience dilemmas of control and time. As noted by Goodfellow et al. (2001), students may struggle with clinical educators' needs or preferences to exert control over them, perhaps believing themselves to be more independently competent than perceived by their clinical educators, or resenting the level of scrutiny exerted by some clinical educators. They may fail to understand that clinical educators do this in order to fulfil their responsibilities for client care.

One emotion experienced by students that is discussed in the literature is that of anxiety (Stengelhofen, 1993; Chan et al., 1994; Alsop and Ryan, 1996; Lincoln et al., 1997a). Chan et al. (1994) studied factors identified by novice, intermediate and entry level students in an Australian speech–language pathology programme. The top 10 factors for each group are shown in Table 4.4. This rank ordering reveals some factors common across all years of students, including time pressures and concerns about whether theoretical and practical knowledge is adequate to provide client care. High expectation for self was common, as was anxiety about making errors in client care. Beginning level students were more concerned with technical aspects of preparing and delivering therapy to clients, whereas final year students were more concerned with factors that threatened their emerging professional identity and control. These results suggest that anxiety for students in clinical education is a combination of intrinsic and extrinsic factors.

Table 4.4 Top 10 factors contributing to student anxiety about clinical placements

Rank	Novice student	Intermediate level student	Entry level student
1	Ability to fulfil both university and clinical demands	Ability to fulfil both university and clinical demands	Ability to fulfil both university and clinical demands
2	Amount of preparation required for clinic	High expectations of myself	Amount of preparation required for clinic
3	Amount of relevant clinical experience	Possibility of making errors in diagnosis	High expectations of myself
4	Possibility of making errors in diagnosis	Level of relevant theoretical knowledge	The fact that I am being assessed
5	Setting therapy goals	Amount of relevant clinical experience	Degree of control that I have in clinic
6	Level of relevant theoretical knowledge	Possibility of making errors while treating clients	Amount of relevant clinical experience
7	Perceived responsibility for total client management	Ability to apply theory to practice	Ability to apply theory to practice
8	Possibility of making errors while treating clients	Setting therapy goals	Clients' disorder type (e.g. developmental disability, voice disorder)
9	Ability to apply theory to practice	Clients' disorder type (e.g. developmental disability, voice disorder)	System of evaluation of students' clinical competence
10	High expectations of myself	Amount of preparation required for clinic	Clarity of clinical educator's expectations

Adapted from Chan et al. (1994)

Strategies for managing emotions in self and others

We have found that strategies for avoiding or managing our emotions and those of others can be grouped into four areas, as listed in Table 4.5.

Table 4.5 Strategies for managing your own emotions and those of others

---

Be aware of 'games'

Use assertive communication

Avoid or manage emotional labour

Set (and monitor) realistic expectations

Students and clinical educators can become ensnared in a number of games within the supervisory context (Kadushin, 1968; Sleight, 1984), as can all humans in interaction (Berne, 1966). The 'poor me' (also known as the 'I've got too much to do') game and the 'assessment is not for friends' game are ones likely to be familiar to many clinical educators. In this first game, students invite sympathy and pity for their circumstances, perhaps hoping that they will obtain a reduction in expectations placed on them. In the second game, one that in our experience is often entered into unknowingly, students and clinical educators establish a friendship that may extend beyond the placement site. This can make it difficult later to provide honest assessment and feedback to each other, for fear of hurting the other, their 'friend'. We are not suggesting that clinical educators and students should not be 'friendly' to each other, but do suggest that the development of 'friendships' during placements be avoided. Students will recognize the 'one good question deserves another' game, where legitimate questions to their clinical educators receive not the required or at least desired information, but another question turned on the student.

Games can be entered into knowingly or unknowingly. They can be used to maintain power or to avoid authenticity and honest interactions. Where students or clinical educators are experiencing what Drake and Irurita (1997) refer to as ambiguity during fieldwork placements, this is often the result of unacknowledged game playing. With game playing comes a host of other emotions, including resentment, anger, powerlessness and anxiety. Clear and if necessary assertive communication, such as that discussed earlier in the chapter, can help expose unproductive games, manage emotions and build a healthier learning relationship.

Managing anxiety and other emotions that arise in the course of clinical placements can lead to emotional labour and, if unduly sustained, to burnout. Emotional labour can be managed by using a number of strategies, including: reduction in factors that lead to fatigue; ensuring that students and clinical educators have some privacy during the working day; providing opportunities for reflection and debriefing on challenging experiences; and allowing expression of negative emotions. As noted earlier, students and clinical educators experience fatigue as they seek to juggle numerous roles. Students also experience information overload at the start of placements. Fatigue can be reduced by providing written briefing material and reference manuals, reducing travel time to and from placements if possible, allowing preparation and report writing time during the clinical day, and encouraging students (and clinical educators) to lead a balanced lifestyle and obtain sufficient rest. When people are not fatigued, the emotional roller-coaster of clinical placements can be seen in perspective and better managed.

Much emotional labour can be prevented in clinical education settings if clinical educators and students mutually establish clear and realistic expectations of each other. These need to be established at the start of placements and reset throughout. Unrealistic expectations create anxiety, fatigue and even anger. Students and clinical educators also benefit from having some level of privacy to experience and deal with adverse emotions that they may feel. They also need a private space to prepare or complete administrative tasks without being under the scrutiny of other people. When negative emotions do arise, after a period of reflection, students and clinical educators alike may find it helpful to be able to cathart or debrief to others. Peers or critical friends can help sort through issues, so that interactions between students and clinical educators can be more focused and clear. They can also help prepare their colleagues for assertive communications or confrontation if required.

Management of tasks and time

Clinical educators fulfil several roles, as described in Chapter 1. They also have multiple responsibilities: to clients, students, colleagues, administrators and so on. They need to learn to balance their roles and responsibilities, in other words to manage the dilemma of purpose described by Edwards (1996), and to juggle their attention and tasks. Given that clinical educators constantly experience dilemmas of time (Brammer, 1996; Edwards, 1996; McAllister, 2001):

> . . . there is never enough time; how will I fit everything in?; who should have priority over my time at this moment?

clinical educators need to develop time management skills. They also need to learn to manage the dilemma of control (Edwards, 1996) and exert appropriate levels of control over students in order to ensure that tasks assigned to students are completed. This can be achieved through appropriately assertive communication, and by effective time management.

Students also need to develop time management skills. Student lives are demanding. Many of them work a high number of hours each week, often in demanding, responsible jobs (McInnis et al., 2000; Lincoln and Aron, 2001). They seek to juggle social lives and community involvement with relationships with families, friends and partners (McInnis et al., 2000). As the number of mature students in the health professions increases (Pickering and McAllister, 1997), many will also be juggling parental duties with study, work commitments and relationships. Students need to manage their time well but are often not good at doing so (Lincoln et al., 2003).

There are many factors that could potentially influence how well students are able to manage their time. As discussed previously, study as well as life demands can combine to reduce the amount of time available to students for their clinical commitments. Richard et al. (1999) suggest that there are several factors that influence how well people manage time. These factors are summarized in Table 4.6.

Table 4.6 Time management dimensions of Richard et al. (1999)

Factor	Explanation	Prompts
Sense of purpose	Refers to an individual's sense of purpose, level of focus and goal-setting capacity	I am driven to achieve my goals I focus on what really matters
Meeting deadlines	Refers to a tendency to procrastinate and the extent which people perceive themselves in control of time, as well as the ability to realistically estimate the time it takes to complete a task	I leave things to the last minute I underestimate the time required to complete a task
Mechanics of time management	Behaviours and actions associated with time management, including using a diary, making a to-do list and adhering to a schedule	I wake up each morning and check my diary I write a daily to-do list
Coping with temporal flow	Refers to an individual's ability to cope with change in the short and long term	I can't cope with change I worry about what the future holds
Propensity to plan	Refers to whether an individual is focused on long-term goals or is easily distracted into pursuing more immediate spontaneous goals.	I like to 'live on the edge' I don't plan things, I just do them
Effective organization	Refers to the level of organization of an individual's workspace	I keep my desk uncluttered I feel relaxed surrounded by mess

It is evident from Table 4.6 that poor time management may not simply result from students' failure to use diaries, timetables and 'to-do' lists. These authors suggest that other factors such as students' abilities to realistically estimate how long tasks will take, their ability and desire to set goals and work towards them, as well as their motivation for being in clinic, may potentially influence their time management abilities. It is also worth noting that the presence of illness or disability may influence time management abilities, e.g. students experiencing depression or chronic fatigue syndrome may find it hard to concentrate for long periods of time, and may require more sleep than normal and therefore reduce the time they have available for study. Another potential factor to consider is the cultural background of the student. In some cultures, lateness and loose time frames are the norm and are acceptable – indeed expected. In our experience, time management difficulties may be the consequence of many different underlying issues for students. Helping students to identify and work on the issues can allow positive change in their skills in this area.

Time management for both clinical educators and students is a developmental skill. Students can be assisted to acquire the necessary skills throughout their clinical education programmes by staging requirements and gradually increasing expectations. Table 4.7 contains an example of an attempt to gradually increase requirements and expectations across a clinical education programme and into the first few years of work.

As mature adults and experienced clinicians, clinical educators are often surprised to find time management as a clinical educator problematic and stressful. Learning to manage yourself and your clients is one thing, adding into the mix students and their multiple needs is quite another. Clinical educators resort to a range of strategies to help organize themselves and their students, such as those listed in Table 4.8.

Although these are excellent strategies, they need to occur within a larger framework of organization for placements. The teacher as manager model was presented in Chapter 2 as one way of helping clinical educators see their role as that of manager of student learning programmes, and defining the stages and tasks required in a learning programme. A well-thought-out, planned, resourced and structured placement will help clinical educators manage their time and themselves more effectively.

Regardless of how well students and clinical educators know themselves and how well organized they may be, the job of managing relationships, time and tasks will remain a complex one, because of the complexity and number of variables and participants in the clinical education setting. It is not possible to control all variables, but it is possible to strive for what McAllister (2001) calls dynamic self-congruence as a means of personal development and management in the clinical education setting. This is discussed briefly in the next section.

Table 4.7 Strategies for supporting the development of time management skills in students

Level of experience	Expectation	Important skills
Novice student	Competent time management within clinical sessions	Estimating length of activities Organization of materials so activities change quickly Starting and finishing on time
Intermediate level student	Competent time management across a clinical day	Using a diary Prioritizing a to-do list Daily schedule that includes time to do all high-priority tasks Contingency planning for cancellations or changes within sessions Adhering to schedule and not being distracted on to less relevant but perhaps enjoyable tasks
Entry level student	Competent time management across a clinical week or placement	Setting and working towards achieving the goals of the placement for themselves and the client Improving abilities in estimating how long it will take to complete a task Not procrastinating Developing a professional attitude to meeting deadlines Coping with changes in workload over time, using down time productively
New graduate	Competent time management across weeks, months	Planning ahead into the future months Developing a longer-term perspective on caseload and workload management Entering monthly and yearly events in a diary Using 'warning' entries for approaching tasks that need to be completed Breaking large tasks down into smaller ones and scheduling time to complete each small task Having a well-organized workspace that promotes efficiency

Table 4.8 Some time management strategies used by clinical educators

Provide a thorough orientation to the clinic and its procedures

Have a comprehensive policy and procedures manual for the clinic and the placement

Develop learning contracts with students

Document procedures for management of paperwork

Set clear written timelines for the submission of reports, file notes and other paperwork

Ask students to book time with you to review plans, files, receive feedback, etc. (rather than being asked to do this in ad hoc ways)

Have a common diary and record all commitments of both clinical educator and students (with clients, clinical educator, team members, case conferences, student conferences, etc.) and times for planning, feedback, file writing times, etc., in the clinical educator's diary (so that they can see at a glance the possible time demands required for that day or week)

Seeking dynamic self-congruence: an important approach to personal development in clinical educators and students

McAllister (2001) identified an approach used by clinical educators to manage themselves and their students, which she labelled 'seeking dynamic self-congruence'. This construct focuses on congruence within yourself as a clinical educator, as you seek to create congruence between your sense of self, sense of self in relationship, sense of being a clinical educator and sense of agency. It is important to note also that the construct refers to 'seeking' rather than 'achieving', and to a dynamic state rather than a static one. No one ever achieves a steady state of being as a clinical educator. The complex dynamic nature of the clinical education environment and the transactional nature of the interactions between participants call for constant readjustments and fine-tuning. Three elements make up this construct:

1. Bringing a higher level of awareness to the role
2. Drawing the selves together
3. Striving for plan–action congruence.

The section below considers how clinical educators might bring a higher level of awareness to their role and the impact that this can have on drawing the selves together, and striving for action–plan congruence.

Bringing a higher level of awareness to the role

This element is made up of two levels of awareness: cognitive awareness and emotional awareness. Cognitive awareness involves awareness of thoughts and thinking processes, in other words metacognition. Emotional awareness involves 'gut feelings' and 'intuition', emotional intelligence (Gilligan, 1993; Goleman, 1995), and sensing 'the flow' of events (Csikszentmihalyi, 1990). In the study by McAllister (2001), the level of awareness apparent in clinical educators varied between heightened awareness, where participants actively monitored or 'reflected in action' to achieve congruence in the midst of being and doing, to 'reflection on action', where participants became aware of congruence or incongruence only after the event or action. Various factors affected the level of awareness brought by clinical educators to the seeking of dynamic self-congruence, including experience, reflective skills, fatigue, proximity, anxiety, whether or not a student was problematic, and the complexity of the task to be monitored. It is suggested that a similar set of factors would apply to students. Indeed, as Nemeth (2004) shows, maturity, fatigue, competence and the perceived level of difficulty of their clinical educator all seem to affect students' abilities to monitor what is happening and manage their relationships with their clinical educators.

We have already discussed development of clinical educators and students from self-focused to other focused as a result of experience and reflection. As this development occurs, they will be aware not only of what they are thinking and feeling but also of what the other person in an interaction may be thinking and feeling. Jenny, the novice clinical educator described in Vignette 4.1, spoke of 'not consciously thinking a lot about what I am doing – it just unfolds'. Emma (Vignette 4.2) noted:

> . . . how my degree of conscious awareness of what I'm thinking and doing during the moment to moment was variable. . . . It wasn't a full consciousness but it wasn't totally unconscious . . . I guess after the event when I'd reflect on what was happening it would come between 90 to 100 per cent.

However, Emma consistently brought heightened emotional awareness to her work, in the form of 'gut feeling' and sensing the emotions of her students, e.g. she spoke of 'the anxiety I'm sensing from Jane', and of 'Katie trailing around in her cloud of anxiety'. Emma's heightened awareness allowed her to track the nuances of interactions in order to judge how to manage that interaction.

Sometimes, use of reflection on action and emotional awareness lead to cognitive awareness. Emma described the experience of 'things in the boiling pot in terms of trying to figure out what's happening and ideas bubbling up' to consciousness. In contrast, Annette (Vignette 4.5) described herself as more instinctive. She found she could:

> . . . let things happen in my subconscious and that I don't need to be involved with close supervision to monitor things – I think picking up on cues is another way of knowing when to step in and step back.

Robyn (Vignette 4.3) talked of her heightened awareness as being able to see 'when there's a particular flow in her [the student's] therapy'.

Students can also aim to bring heightened awareness to their clinical work and interactions with clinical educators. John, in Vignette 4.7, was able to identify why he was feeling both excitement and apprehension about his pending school visit, whereas Trudi was unaware of why she felt exhausted after each clinical session. In Vignette 4.8, Sue was aware of the impact of her clinical educator's collegial style of supervision on her own professional growth and development. Bringing a higher level of awareness to one's work facilitates drawing the selves together.

Drawing the selves together

Clinical educators who participated in the study with McAllister (2001) expressed a desire for authenticity, sensitivity, empathy and caring in relationships with others, and for generally collaborative, flexible approaches to clinical education. These are values and attributes that we would hope our students also demonstrate. The clinical educators sought congruence between how they saw themselves as people and how others saw them, e.g. Emma (see Vignette 4.2) worried about doing 'anything that was detrimental to her [student's] character, to her self-esteem. She did not want to be seen as insensitive to her needs'.

As a result of challenging interactions with her failing students, and her state of burnout, Annette (Vignette 4.5) often experienced anxiety and frustration; however, she thought it important 'to try to be natural' in order to create a relaxed learning environment for her students and to maintain supportive relationships. As a result, she felt that she was not true to herself, she was not authentic with the students – she 'did not like what she saw herself doing'. By way of contrast, Ann (Vignette 4.4) felt that she was able to draw her various selves together, creating what she referred to as 'personal and professional circle fulfilment'. As a result of life and work experience, critical reflection and counselling, Ann felt that she knew who she was. By bringing a high level of attention to her interactions with people, Ann more often achieved dynamic self-congruence of who she was, what she valued in relationships and her approaches to being a clinical educator.

It could be argued that students are also attempting to achieve dynamic self-congruence through integration of their personal self with their professional self. Students often talk positively about clinical educators who 'take the time to get to know them as people' and are 'interested in their lives'. These clinical educators are encouraging students to bring their personal selves into the professional domain. In Vignette 4.7, John has also found a way to use his personal interests effectively in treatment. Another example of students seeking dynamic self-congruence is when they experiment with the manner in which they dress in the clinical setting. Finding the right balance between asserting their personal identity through dress and meeting society's norm and expectations about how professionals should dress can be challenging for some students.

Learning exercise 4.3: self-evaluating self-congruence

Think of a time when you felt that you had been incongruent or in some way untrue to yourself and your values within the clinical education context. What was the situation? Where did it occur? Who was involved? What were you thinking and feeling at the time? What values were in conflict for you? What factors might have contributed to this incongruence? What did you do to try to right the incongruence? How might you avoid similar situations in the future?

Striving for plan–action congruence

As well as seeking congruence of the inner self, self in relationship and self as clinical educator, participants in the study with McAllister (2001) also sought to create self-congruence between desired approaches to clinical education and what was actually implemented. They strove for congruence between the goals, objectives and planned approaches, and the strategies applied and actions taken to achieve these. Striving for plan–action congruence implies reflecting on congruence between aspirations and actions, and deliberately seeking out feedback or acting on opportunistic feedback to maintain self-congruence, redress incongruence, and reduce the gap between espoused theory and theory in action (Argyris and Schön, 1974). Both cognitive awareness and emotional awareness are used, and awareness of plan–action (in)congruence can arise in action, or upon reflection.

Emma (Vignette 4.2) clearly articulated the experience of deliberate monitoring during interactions to ensure congruence of actions and words with intention. As she wanted to show respect and sensitivity for students and to support their personal and professional growth, Emma felt she 'always needed to quite consciously be aware of what I say and how I interact [with students]'. She often spoke on different occasions of:

> . . . being conscious of being directive, being conscious that I reflect back [to the student] rather than give the answer, being quite consciously aware of how the student reacted, being very conscious of what feedback I write to the student.

In spite of quite deliberate attempts, Emma did not always achieve the dynamic self-congruence she desired. She recounted the experience of giving a student her mid-placement assessment, which was quite positive but with a few comments on things to improve, and watching the student become extremely anxious. She thought 'oh no, what have I done'. Given student propensity for perfectionism and anxiety discussed earlier, this lack of plan–action congruence was perhaps something unavoidable, even with heightened self-knowledge and self-awareness. Ann (Vignette 4.4) was particularly committed to striving for self-congruence between her desired collaborative approach to clinical education and actions. She talked of being aware of whether she was:

> . . . retaining power or control, playing games. I really don't want to be like that, it doesn't at all match my philosophy of what I was trying to do or who I am as a person.

With the less experienced clinical educators, the achievement of plan–action congruence was often serendipitous rather than the product of deliberate striving for congruence. They might become aware of congruence as they reflected on outcomes of the actions taken, e.g. while discussing student progress, Jenny thought back to actions she had taken with her student:

> . . . looking back, you realise it's effective when you match your student's style rather than your own. You can actually see effectiveness because you are doing it their way.

There has been no investigation of how students strive for congruence between plans and actions, but experience tells us that many factors make it hard for them to achieve this congruence. Being self-focused rather than other focused, anxiety, lack of confidence and poor time management are all likely to be factors that impact on plan–action incongruence, e.g. because of lack of confidence in the professional role, students may shy away from providing clients or their family members with direct feedback on behaviour. A young student may plan to tell a mother that her monopolization of talking time with her child is serving to maintain a passive communication style, but may be unable to actually deliver this input because of lack of confidence and a perceived lack of credibility. Another student may recognize that her clinical educator's overly direct style of supervision is hampering her development of independence and plan to tell her this, politely but clearly, next time they have a post-session conference. Fear of adverse assessment may lead to the student not being able to say what he or she thinks and needs, even when the clinical educator asks for feedback on how things are going.

Conclusion

The likelihood of drawing the selves together and achieving plan–action congruence is enhanced if clinical educators and students deliberately adopt strategies to help them achieve these things. Making time for reflection on action and seeking feedback from others, including one's clinical educators and students, can make the quest of striving for dynamic self-congruence more attainable, e.g. Emma (Vignette 4.2), as well as writing about her experiences, reports how she liked 'to take time to just think with no interruptions and be by myself and ask myself questions in my head and just go through the motions of what I experienced and what was going on and what I'm going to do for the next time'. Annette (Vignette 4.5) also used planned reflection time. She would 'video something and look at it and think oh my goodness we could have done that better, or something else works better'. However, more often reflection occurred in unplanned ways. The value of reflection is enhanced when it occurs in a planned way (Boud et al., 1985).

In striving for congruence between intentions and actions, the participants in McAllister's (2001) study all deliberately sought feedback from others, most frequently from their students, to help them achieve congruence between aspirations and actions. Annette deliberately sought feedback from her students: 'when we do the mid-placement assessment and when we do the . . . appraisal. I say that I'm still learning too and that I need feedback.' Jenny sought feedback from her student on her supervision: 'we spoke last week about the feedback, was she getting enough, and she said "yes the feedback's great, you give as much positive as negative and suggestions for things I could work on".'

Emma, Jenny and Annette all described seeking feedback from other clinical educators about their approaches, e.g. Annette described 'feeling fairly isolated out here and ringing [a colleague] and saying, look, can we just talk this through'. When it was time to complete her first assessment of her student, Jenny asked two colleagues 'would you be happy if you got an assessment report that looked like that?', as she did not want to upset the student's growing confidence or damage her relationship with her.

Just as it is for novice clinical educators, striving for dynamic self-congruence is a challenging task for students. As a result of maturity levels and their novice status, much of students' cognitive and emotional awareness in the clinical setting is self-focused. They may not have the spare capacity needed to heighten attention and monitor whether they are being self-congruent or achieving what they set out to do. Learning to do these things is a major learning goal for them throughout their clinical education. Clinical educators can assist students to achieve a drawing together of their selves and plan–action congruence by role-modelling and discussing the approaches that they use to seek dynamic self-congruence. The learning strategies of reflection and seeking feedback are discussed further in Chapter 6.

CHAPTER 5

Development of cognitive skills

In Chapter 1 we argued that clinical education offers both clinical educators and students opportunities for professional and personal development. Chapter 4 discussed the nature of personal development in students and clinical educators, illustrating the roles that each could play in supporting personal growth in the other. This chapter considers the development of cognitive skills, again arguing that both clinical educators and students can support the development of cognitive skills in themselves and each other within the context of a learning relationship in the clinical education setting.

This chapter addresses four areas of cognitive skill:

1. Different types of knowledge
2. Different approaches to reasoning
3. Clinical reasoning
4. Ethical reasoning.

Types of knowledge

Put simply, knowledge is the information that individual clinicians hold, select and apply when making clinical decisions. According to Higgs and Titchen (2000), three overlapping and interactive types of knowledge are held by clinicians: propositional knowledge, professional craft knowledge and personal knowledge. A fourth aspect of knowledge to be considered is that of tacit knowledge (Polyani, 1958).

Propositional knowledge

Propositional knowledge is often referred to as 'textbook' knowledge. It is theoretical and abstract knowledge generated by research and scholarship in one's discipline. It is this type of knowledge that beginning student clinicians take to clinic. The clinical setting requires that students transform and develop this type of knowledge into professional craft knowledge.

Professional craft knowledge

Higgs and Titchen (2000) use this term to refer to types of non-propositional knowledge within professional domains. Professional craft knowledge encompasses procedural knowledge (Biggs and Telfer, 1987) and practical knowledge (Benner, 1984), i.e. how to get things done in the clinical setting, as opposed to how textbooks say things should be done. Professional craft knowledge accommodates the particularities and idiosyncrasies of clinical settings and client needs, and requires propositional knowledge to be transformed in specific, clinically relevant ways. Professional craft knowledge also incorporates the 'wisdom' and 'talent' considered by Schön (1987) and Fish and colleagues (Fish and Twinn, 1997; Fish and Coles, 1998) to characterize professional artistry. In addition, clinical judgement and clinical intuition (McCormack, 1992) can be seen as components of professional craft knowledge.

Personal knowledge

Higgs and Titchen (2000) define personal knowledge as 'the unique frame of reference and knowledge of self which is central to the individual's sense of self' (p. 28). Aspects of sense of self, as they relate to clinical educators and students, were discussed in Chapter 4, and the importance of developing self-knowledge was considered in Chapter 3.

Tacit knowledge

Tacit knowledge is the body of professional knowledge that experts possess, which is not processed in a 'focused cognitive manner but rather lies at a not quite conscious level' (Hayes Fleming and Mattingly, 2000, p. 55). Tacit knowledge is not easily verbalized but can be accessed in the process of judging and doing. In a process of sustained engagement with critical companions (Titchen, 2001) or researchers (Clandinin and Connelly, 1994; McAllister, 2001), tacit knowledge can be uncovered and articulated by experts. Questions asked by students can help clinicians and clinical educators bring their embedded, tacit knowledge to the surface, thus supporting the cognitive development of their educators. Similarly, clinical educators' questions can help students articulate their tacit knowledge.

The development of knowledge types is likely to be influenced by many factors. Professional socialization is an important influence; observation of the knowledge that others hold and how they apply it to the clinical situation conveys information about what type of knowledge is considered most valid. Professional experiences also play an important role in building up professional craft knowledge (Cusick, 2001). Our early life experiences also shape who we are as people. These early life experiences are influenced by many factors, including gender (Belenky et al., 1986; Severiens and Ten Dam, 1998) and class (Weiler, 1988). These in turn influence the way we reason.

Influences on reasoning

Belenky et al. (1986) and Gilligan (1993) argue that females view the construction and acquisition of knowledge differently to males. Baxter Magolda (1992) found that women use different patterns of reasoning to men, characterized by a focus on relational aspects. Women seem to be more open to other perspectives and will tend to incorporate other perspectives into their own. Males are more likely to be self-focused on their learning processes and perspectives. Women may make decisions that consider the impact of the decisions on the people involved. Men may make decisions based primarily on propositional knowledge, or on simplistic right/wrong dichotomies (Perry, 1970). Philosophers such as Noddings (1984, 1991) believe that such gender differences in interpersonal reasoning lead to differences in approaches to caring, an important aspect of the work of health professionals.

It is important that clinical educators and students both understand the potential impact of gender on their individual approaches to reasoning. Women dominate the speech pathology profession: in Australia the ratio is 97% female:3% male (Speech Pathology Association of Australia or SPAA, 2002a); in the UK the figure is similar. For many of these women, knowledge will often be constructed in the context of relationships, and reasoning will consider relationship issues. Those few men who do enter the profession may experience highly feminized ways of developing and using knowledge and reasoning skills. This may be a factor in attrition from student cohorts and from the profession itself (Farmer and Farmer, 1989). Furthermore, given that most clients of speech–language pathologists are male, the feminization of the profession may have impacts on the nature of goals, role-modelling and interaction during service delivery. Such gender differences may also impact on how clinical reasoning is developed and applied.

Other factors also impact on clinical reasoning (Higgs and Jones, 2000). When clinicians are under time pressure or are not motivated to consider all options, their reasoning may not be comprehensive in scope.

Further, individuals' personal frames of reference (Cusick, 2001) may interfere with seeing alternative perspectives on clients' problems. As a result, clinicians' decisions may be inadequate or even wrong. In addition, effective clinical reasoning requires a rich, well-organized knowledge base (Patel et al., 1990; Schmidt et al., 1990). Students or clinicians working in new areas, or with unusual client types for whom they do not yet have the requisite knowledge, may be inefficient or ineffective in their clinical reasoning. Students particularly may have the required propositional knowledge but not be able to transfer it into professional craft knowledge applicable to a particular client or to a particular context. Finally, clinicians and students who do not monitor their thinking routinely, i.e. use metacognitive strategies to monitor and challenge their assumptions, thought processes and outcomes, may also find that their clinical reasoning is not adequate.

Clinical reasoning in speech–language pathology

McAllister and Rose (2000) report an absence in the speech–language pathology literature of discussion on clinical reasoning. This is in marked contrast to medicine, physiotherapy, occupational therapy and nursing, where research and discussion of clinical reasoning abound, and clinical reasoning is an explicit part of many curricula (see Higgs and Jones, 2000). Speech–language pathologists discuss and write about differential diagnosis (Dodd, 1995), and diagnostic or clinical decision-making (see, for example, an entire issue of Seminars in Speech and Language, 1998).

McAllister and Rose (2000) offered reasons for a lack of discussion of clinical reasoning as including:

• Adoption of a content-oriented approach which assumes that knowledge and reasoning are interdependent, and that increasing knowledge and clinical experience will ensure increasing clinical reasoning ability.
• A focus on problem-solving (i.e. the outcome), not the process of thinking about problems.
• An assumption that clinical decision-making in speech–language pathology is linear and logical, not messy and circular. Decision-making trees (e.g. those of Yoder and Kent, 1988) are an outcome of such an assumption.

This is not to say speech–language pathologists do not use clinical reasoning; they do, but they have not seen it as a topic for research and scholarship. As a result, we have no 'language' for thinking about and discussing it. Consequently, this chapter borrows the language of other health disciplines to discuss approaches to clinical reasoning and how clinical educators and students jointly might develop their clinical reasoning skills.

Approaches to clinical reasoning

Higgs and Jones (2000), in reviewing the clinical education literature from a range of health professions, discuss nine approaches to clinical reasoning. These are presented in Table 5.1.

Table 5.1 Approaches to clinical reasoning in health professionals

Hypothetico-deductive reasoning

Pattern recognition

Knowledge–reasoning integration

Interactive reasoning

Narrative reasoning

Collaborative reasoning

Predictive or conditional reasoning

Ethical/pragmatic reasoning

Integrated patient-centred reasoning

Hypothetico-deductive reasoning

This view of clinical reasoning comes from medicine (Barrows and Feltovich, 1987; Elstein et al., 1978), where it is assumed that doctors generate hypotheses derived from clinical data, observations and knowledge, and seek to test, confirm, eliminate or generate alternate hypotheses based on further inquiry. It is used in diagnostic reasoning (Albert et al., 1988). This approach to clinical reasoning has also been noted in nursing (Padrick et al., 1987), occupational therapy (Fleming, 1991) and physiotherapy (Jones, 1992). We would suggest that it also operates in speech–language pathology, particularly in medical settings and particularly with novices. Experienced clinicians may revert to this approach when faced with unusually complex or unfamiliar presentations.

Pattern recognition

This approach to clinical reasoning is faster than hypothetico-deductive reasoning, but requires a mental bank of 'patterns' or typical, prototype, clinical presentations which are built up through clinical experience. As such it is not an approach that is accurately used by novices. Clinicians from all health professions appear to use this approach, including speech–language pathologists.

Knowledge–reasoning integration

This approach acknowledges that clinical reasoning is not a skill that can be developed separately from a rich, well-organized knowledge base (Patel et al., 1990; Schmidt et al., 1990). Clinical reasoning skills develop in parallel with cognitive skills such as critical, creative, reflective and analytical thinking, and metacognition, and with the development of knowledge. As noted earlier, speech–language pathology education emphasizes building knowledge and decision-making abilities; it does not often, however, explicitly emphasize the development of metacognitive skills.

Recent work in occupational therapy (Mattingly and Hayes-Fleming, 1994) and in physiotherapy (Edwards et al., 1998) has revealed a number of different approaches to clinical reasoning in those professions. The work from occupational therapy is particularly salient in speech–language pathology, given that, as in occupational therapy, we work in rehabilitation settings with clients for prolonged periods helping them to recreate a new meaning and direction for life after illness or injury. Our recent adoption of a social model of disability (Duchan, 2001) as a framework for professional practice will also require us to use more of what Higgs and Titchen (2000) call interpretive models of clinical reasoning, where we accept multiple interpretations of events, and structure meaning and interpret a problem from the patient's perspective.

Interactive reasoning

In this approach, social exchanges between client and professional are used to enhance the assessment and management of a client. Dialogue helps create and maintain a supportive relationship between client and professional, and allows the health professional to come to understand the client's problems, context and world view. Speech–language pathologists are very likely to use this approach to clinical reasoning, given their skill in using social exchanges as both a means to, and an end of, the therapeutic process.

Narrative reasoning

Narratives are often embedded in social interactions between humans. Hayes-Fleming and Mattingly (2000) suggest that, when occupational therapists engage in narrative reasoning, they use the narratives embedded in interaction with clients to organize clinical problems and treatments in their minds as an unfolding drama. The aspects of story grammar familiar to speech–language pathologists come into play, in that 'a cast of characters emerges'. Motives are inferred or examined. Narrative reasoning is needed when clinicians want to understand concrete events that cannot be comprehended without relating a client's inner world of desire and motive to their outer world of observable actions and states of affairs. Narrative reasoning is concerned with the relationship between motives, actions and consequences as these play out in some specific situation (Hayes Fleming and Mattingly, 2000). Teachers also use narrative reasoning with their students (Connelly and Clandinin, 1988), as do clinical educators with their students (McAllister, 2001). Narrative reasoning allows professionals to enter the old or newly constructed life story of their client or student undergoing significant life change or development, to understand their world view, motives and aspirations. We would suggest that narrative reasoning is also used by speech–language pathologists who actively seek to understand the emotional and physical worlds of clients whom they come to know over periods of therapy.

Collaborative reasoning

This approach to clinical reasoning differs from interactive reasoning discussed earlier, in that it explicitly involves shared decision-making between client and professional. The opinions of clients or their significant others, as well as information about the presenting problem, are sought and used in reasoning and decision-making processes. Involvement of clients and their significant others in decision-making and management planning is a requirement in the competency standards for speech–language pathologists in Australia (SPAA, 2001), and we would suggest that collaborative reasoning is used extensively.

Predictive or conditional reasoning

In this approach to clinical reasoning the professional estimates the likely client response to, and outcomes of, treatment. The clinician uses a range of information in this reasoning process. We would suggest that effective conditional reasoning requires some ability in hypothetico-deductive reasoning and pattern recognition, in this case for outcomes, and not clinical presentation as described above.

Ethical/pragmatic reasoning

Higgs and Jones (2000) describe this approach as alluding to 'those less recognised but frequently made decisions regarding moral, political and economic dilemmas which clinicians regularly confront, such as deciding how long to continue treatment' (p. 8). All clinicians engage in ethical reasoning, and frameworks for assisting clinicians and students to develop this type of reasoning are discussed later in this chapter.

Professionals most probably use a range of approaches to clinical reasoning depending on experience, the context and the client presentation. The scenarios in Vignette 5.1 illustrate students and clinicians at different stages of their professional development. What type of clinical reasoning approach do you think each person is using?

Vignette 5.1: students and clinicians using different approaches to clinical reasoning

Kate was in her first placement in an acute medical setting. She accompanied her clinical educator John while he conducted an informal bedside evaluation of a newly referred client with aphasia. When asked her opinion on what she thought was the nature of the client's speech and language problems, Kate was hesitant and expressed confusion. She said that some of the client's responses looked like a client with an expressive aphasia, but that other responses suggested a more Wernicke type of aphasia. She said that the client didn't fit with anything she had learned about in her aphasia class. When John asked her what she would do to make a diagnosis of the type of aphasia so that an intervention plan could be developed, Kate said she would test first of all for Broca's aphasia, and then, if the tests didn't show that, she would test for something else.

John, Kate's clinical educator, was in no doubt at all that this was a Broca type of aphasia. He had worked in acute medical settings for several years now, and had seen many clients with this type of problem. Even though the client wasn't a 'classic textbook type case', he recognized the core features of Broca's aphasia.

Sally was a final year student in her final placement in a community paediatric placement. She had planned a full speech and language assessment of a 3-year-old child referred for being 'slow to talk'. During play she noted that the child had few words and very short utterances. She also noticed that the child watched her face intently as she talked while they were sitting at a table doing a puzzle, but appeared to ignore her while she was playing at the doll's house with her back to Sally. Sally's second year clinical placement had been at the local school for hearing-impaired children, and Sally had seen this type of behaviour with preschoolers who had not long been aided. Sally wondered whether the child she was assessing had a hearing loss, and if this was the reason for her delayed language development. She referred the child for priority hearing evaluation.

Jane has been working in an adult rehab facility for many years. She has been working with Peter, a 22-year-old who had sustained a traumatic brain injury after a motorcycle accident. Peter is making slow progress in rehab. He is depressed and not motivated really to participate in speech and language therapy. Jane has a son of Peter's age and knows the sorts of interests that 22-year-old men might have. One day she manages to get Peter talking about what had been his hobbies, interests and career aspirations before the accident. She finds out that Peter had been planning to go to law school. She spends much time talking with him about where he sees himself heading now with his life, and whether any of his other interests or skills might offer an alternative career choice. Peter maintains that he will recover enough to go to law school next year, but Jane's knowledge of the language demands required for legal practice, and her experience with many clients similar to Peter, suggest to her that she should continue to help Peter realize the extent of his loss and help him think of alternative careers.

We suggest that Kate is most probably using a hypothetico-deductive approach to clinical reasoning. She seems to be hypothesizing a type of aphasia but discounting it because it does not fit the textbook. She then hypotheses something else and plans to test for that, etc. She is relying heavily on propositional knowledge rather than professional craft knowledge at this stage. Her lack of experience with this population means that she has not seen enough clients with aphasia to recognize patterns, unlike her clinical educator John, who sees the 'pattern' amidst the individual variability in the client's presentation. Sally is able to draw on her experience with children with hearing impairment to recognize a behavioural pattern. Jane is using narrative reasoning to enter into her client's past life and future aspirations. She is also using predictive reasoning, drawing on her vast clinical experience, to suggest that her client's recovery will not be sufficient for him to fulfil his career aspirations.

What approaches to clinical reasoning do speech–language pathologists use?

The section above has overviewed several different approaches to clinical reasoning described in the health professions. As noted earlier there appears to have been no research into clinical reasoning in speech–language pathology. However, our experience as educators and clinicians leads us to suggest that speech–language pathologists use all of the above approaches to clinical reasoning depending on the interplay of a range of factors. These factors are listed in Table 5.2.

Table 5.2 Factors influencing clinical reasoning

Depth and breadth of knowledge base

Understanding of personal knowledge and professional craft knowledge brought into context

Amount and diversity of clinical experience

Familiarity with client type or impairment/disorder type

Complexity of client presentation/problem

Degree of involvement of the client in the reasoning process

Preference for technical–rational view of the world versus interpretive world view

Ability to use metacognition

Work context

Where knowledge bases and clinical experience are limited, as in novice clinicians and students, there is likely to be more reliance on hypothetico-deductive reasoning. The more experience and knowledge that we have, the more likely we are to be able to use an array of reasoning approaches, recognize patterns and engage in predictive reasoning. However, experienced clinicians draw on hypothetico-deductive reasoning when faced with complex client problems (Boshuizen and Schmidt, 1992). The more we tend towards an interpretive world view that is sensitive to the experiences of others and acknowledges that people view their worlds differently through different frames of reference, and experience phenomena differently, then perhaps we are more likely to use narrative, interactive and collaborative reasoning. Work setting may also make a difference. As noted earlier, speech–language pathologists working in short-term acute-care settings may rely more on hypothetico-deductive reasoning and pattern recognition. Speech–language pathologists working in rehabilitation or community settings, where they may have extended care relationships with clients and come to know them as people, not patients, may use narrative and collaborative reasoning more frequently.

The important point to make here is that no one mode of clinical reasoning is 'better' or 'right' – it depends on a range of client needs and situational factors. Amidst all the speculation about how speech–language pathologists reason, one thing we can be sure of is that clinical expertise makes a difference to the rate and quality of clinical reasoning and decision-making, and to the clinical reasoning strategies used (Boshuizen and Schmidt, 2000). Glaser and Chi (1988) identified seven characteristics of experts generally, to which Higgs and Jones (2000) added another seven characteristics specific to experts in the health professions. These 14 characteristics are listed in Table 5.3.

Table 5.3 Characteristics of experts

They excel mainly in their own domains

They perceive large meaningful patterns in their domain

They are fast: they are faster than novices at performing the skills of their domain and they quickly solve problems with little error

They have superior short-term and long-term memory

They see and represent a problem in their domain at a deeper (more principled) level than novices; novices tend to represent a problem at a superficial level

They spend a great deal of time analysing a problem qualitatively

They have strong self-monitoring skills

They value the participation of relevant others (e.g. clients, family, team) in decision-making

They use high levels of metacognition in their reasoning

They recognize the value of different forms of knowledge in their reasoning and use this knowledge critically

They are patient centred

They share their expertise to help develop expertise in others

They are able to communicate their reasoning well and in a manner appropriate to their audience

They demonstrate cultural competence in their reasoning and communication

Compiled from Glaser and Chi (1988) and Higgs and Jones (2000).

A model of clinical reasoning that acknowledges the role of factors influencing clinical reasoning outlined above, which incorporates the features of expert practice in Table 5.3, as well as client needs in the reasoning process, is the integrated, patient-centred model of clinical reasoning proposed by Higgs and Jones (2000).

An integrated, patient-centred model of clinical reasoning

This model draws together many facets of the clinical reasoning approaches reviewed above, but also takes into account the more assertive role of the client in healthcare decision-making and service delivery, the diversity of environments in which healthcare needs arise and services are to be delivered (e.g. domiciliary and work settings), and the complex, uncertain, rapidly changing nature of client problems. It is made up of six clinical reasoning elements:

1. Cognition or reflective inquiry
2. A strong discipline-specific knowledge base
3. Metacognition, which provides the integrative element between the knowledge base and cognition
4. The client's input and role in joint decision-making
5. Contextual interaction, acknowledging the role of the environment and situation of the client and decision-making team
6. The impact of the nature of the clinical problem on the reasoning process.

This model provides a useful framework for considering how clinical educators and students can work in parallel to develop each other's clinical reasoning skills.

Promoting parallel development of clinical reasoning in clinical educators and students

One of the debates in the literature on clinical reasoning revolves around where and how best to teach it (Refshauge and Higgs, 2000). Doyle (2000), for example, argues against the teaching of a separate subject on clinical reasoning, such as occurs in many occupational therapy courses, arguing that there is no evidence that such theoretical teaching generalizes to clinical practice. She argues for teaching clinical reasoning in the clinic, or mock clinical settings, e.g. with the use of simulated patients. We suggest that the clinical environment is an ideal place to develop clinical reasoning, because it provides multiple, diverse, ongoing interactions with real clients situated in real, complex environments, with real and immediate needs for such reasoning and decision-making.

Pairing experienced clinicians/clinical educators with novices/students provides a blend of knowledge bases and clinical reasoning approaches that can be applied to a client problem. The strengths of each party can be brought into play to help offset the limitations of the other, e.g. students may have more recent propositional knowledge that can be shared with their clinical educator. However, students tend to have smaller, less integrated personal and professional craft knowledge bases; their clinical educators can bring their greater experience and personal knowledge to clinical problems. As a result of experience, clinical educators may be more adept at identifying subtle environmental and interactional cues, and recognizing the probable impact of the nature of the clinical problem on the reasoning process. Clinical educators can apply these knowledge bases and cues to narrative and collaborative reasoning. Beginning students tend to use more hypothetico-deductive approaches that are slower, but they may be more thorough and open to new hypotheses than their clinical educators who may use faster means of reasoning such as pattern recognition, but who perhaps discount significant information that does not fit 'the pattern'. Students may bring a higher level of metacognition to their reasoning process than their clinical educators. This may be because of the intellectual effort required as a result of students' inexperience in clinical reasoning and coaching received at university, whereas clinical educators may be rushed or on 'auto-pilot'. Alternatively, students may be so overwhelmed by the demands of the client problem, environment and reasoning process, that they cannot monitor their thinking, in which case clinical educators can provide the trigger and framework for doing this.

The number of ways in which clinical educators and students support the development of each other's clinical reasoning will be as varied as the number of clinical educator/student partnerships. Each person will need to understand the other's strengths and weaknesses in clinical reasoning and find ways to complement and strengthen these. This requires a sense of self as discussed in Chapters 1, 3 and 4, strong cognitive skills, and personal skills as described in Chapter 4, and a trusting 'learning relationship' such as that described in Chapter 3. Within the context of such a relationship, students and clinical educators could function for each other as critical companions (Titchen, 2001). Titchen identified four concepts involved in facilitation of learning by critical companions:

1. Consciousness-raising
2. Problematization
3. Self-reflection
4. Critique.

Applying these concepts to the daily business of the clinical setting and clinical education relationship, students and clinical educators can promote each other's clinical reasoning by:

- Making what is taken for granted an object of curiosity or questioning
- Alerting each other to clinical situations that require more thought
- Identifying the nature of the problem
- Sharing their own reflection and reasoning about problems and prompting the reflection and sharing of the other
- Critiquing the knowledge and reasoning used by the other (with sensitivity and respect)

- Contributing new knowledge, perspectives and reasoning about a problem.

To become comfortable doing this may take time, and certainly it will take commitment and role-modelling from the clinical educator. Our experience suggests that speech–language pathologists are not confident in sharing their clinical reasoning with colleagues. One way that this could be developed is to start with reasoning through discussion of case studies of clients seen together in practice by both students and clinical educators. The following provides a template for sharing clinical reasoning that can be transferred to real life, real time contexts as comfort and trust between learning partners grows.

Learning exercise 5.1: discussing your clinical reasoning with your student/clinical educator

Choose a client with whom you have both been involved in assessment. Independently review the referral, case history, assessment results, and your diagnosis, prognosis and programming recommendations. Then meet to discuss each person's answers to the following questions:

1. Try to recall what you were thinking as you read the referral information, chose assessment tools, interpreted results, proposed a diagnosis, made programming recommendations.
2. What appeared salient to you at each step and why?
3. What sorts of knowledge (propositional, personal, professional craft) did you use in reasoning about this client?
4. Did you monitor your thinking, while you were reasoning? After? (i.e. reflect on what you had thought and why)
5. How mutual was the decision-making? Was the client involved as much as possible?
6. Did you thoroughly consider the impact of the client's problem on their life?
7. Did you pay close attention to the context and environment of this client?
8. Did you take into account their history, experiences, aspirations?
9. Review the different approaches to clinical reasoning listed in Table 5.1. Which one(s) did you use? Favour? Prefer? Why?
10. Why did you make the diagnosis you did? How did you arrive at that decision?
11. As you reflect on that diagnosis with the benefit of distance, time and perhaps more information, might you now consider alternative diagnoses? Why?

12. Why did you make the programming recommendations you did? How did you arrive at those recommendations?
13. As you reflect on those recommendations, with the benefit of distance, time and perhaps more information, might you now consider alternative recommendations? Why?

In the exercise above, the differing clinical reasoning approaches of both clinical educators and students will become apparent. The exercise will draw into play the strengths of each partner in the clinical reasoning process, and allow a pooling of knowledge and skills. The exercise forces the clinical educator to engage in a practice that they may rarely do, that of articulating their tacit, personal and professional craft knowledge. As they role-model their reasoning approaches for their student, they are also giving their student opportunities to share their knowledge and reasoning approaches with them.

The next exercise takes less time, but requires greater trust between clinical educator and student. It focuses on the clinical reasoning used in ongoing client management and treatment, unlike the exercise above, and unlike most clinical reasoning literature, which focuses on assessment and diagnosis.

Learning exercise 5.2: exploring your clinical reasoning

1. Obtain a portable video camera with a zoom function.
2. Identify a client whose management you find in some way challenging – theoretically, practically or emotionally – and obtain their permission to video yourself working with them.
3. Set the camera up close enough to get a clear view of you and your client, but far enough away so that your partner's questions and comments off-camera do not distract you or the client. Your partner sits beside the camera out of view of the client if possible.
4. Ask your partner to suspend his or her assumptions about what you are doing and why, and instead identify any points of practice that might be of interest. Have him or her ask questions or make comments aloud (but quietly) as he or she watches you work, along the lines of: 'I wonder why she did that'; 'Why are you doing it this way and not that way?'; 'How is she feeling about what the client is saying/doing here?' These questions and comments will provide useful prompts for discussion when you review the tape.
5. Video 15–30 minutes of your work with the client.
6. Agree with your partner that, when you view the tape, the aim is to

explore your practice and help you understand what you are doing and why, not necessarily to critique it or measure it against 'best practice'.

7. View the video with your partner; stop the tape whenever your partner's questions or comments are heard and try to answer as fully, honestly and self-critically as you can. You can also stop the tape at any other point that seems important or relevant to you.

8. Your partner's role here is to help you get below the surface of what you are doing and saying. If, for example, you comment that 'I did x because of y', your partner might respond with 'but why did you think that was important? Why did you choose to do x and not z?'

9. On another day, reverse roles with your partner. You will learn from this experience in either role.

Adapted from McAllister (2002).

This section has considered clinical reasoning approaches and ways in which students and clinical educators can work in parallel to support the development of each other's clinical reasoning. We have not mentioned ethics as a factor in clinical reasoning, although a consideration of the ethics of any clinical situation is integral to effective clinical reasoning and clinical management. The next section discusses ethical reasoning and provides a template for clinical educators and students to use in the development of clinical reasoning. This protocol could be integrated into any clinical reasoning in which students and their educators are involved.

Ethical reasoning

All professions aim to practise in accordance with a published code of ethics. In the health professions, such codes are typically structured around several ethical principles (Seedhouse and Lovett, 1992). These ethical principles are listed in Table 5.4.

Many codes of ethics are prescriptive, i.e. they attempt to prescribe what members should not do. The approach taken in the revised code of ethics of the Speech Pathology Association of Australia (SPAA) (2000) is aspirational rather than prescriptive. The code prompts members to aspire to ethical conduct and illustrates aspects of such aspirational ethical behaviour in terms of the application of ethics principles and duties towards four groups:

1. Clients and the community
2. Employers
3. The profession at large
4. Colleagues.

Table 5.4 Ethical principles

Beneficence: we seek to benefit others

Non-maleficence: we seek to prevent harm to others

Autonomy: we respect clients' desire to make their own decisions and be independent

Truthfulness: we tell the truth to clients, their families, colleagues and so on

Fidelity: we are faithful, we try to do what we say we will do

Distributive justice: we try to ensure that all our clients, colleagues, etc. have equal access to services, resources, opportunities

Confidentiality: we do not disclose information about our clients or colleagues without their consent

Informed consent: we ensure that our clients fully understand the implications and their rights around giving us information and with whom that might be shared, and we make sure that our clients fully understand the implications of and their rights around participation in services, research, etc. before they agree to participate or receive services

---

The code and its accompanying Ethics Education Package (SPAA, 2002b) acknowledge that, in the complex dynamic environments in which we work, there is sometimes not one clear answer and often there are multiple solutions to ethical dilemmas. Speech–language pathologists are encouraged to learn to reason through ethical dilemmas.

Learning to reason ethically

Learning to understand ethical principles, recognize them at play in ethical dilemmas in the workplace and use them in ethical reasoning is a complex task. Our ability to reason ethically and make ethically sound decisions is undoubtedly a developmental skill, one that we know very little about. Research has not examined this area of our practice. Our clinical experience tells us that experts make ethical decisions faster, with greater cognizance of the factors involved and recognition of the possible impacts on people and services involved. Learning to think through complex situations involving the interests of multiple stakeholders and recognize conflicts between ethical principles can be facilitated by explicit instruction. We have found it useful to provide students and clinicians with protocols for ethical reasoning, and help them apply those to case studies.

An ethical reasoning and decision-making protocol

There are a number of ethical decision-making protocols available (see, for example, Seedhouse and Lovett, 1992; Paul, 2002). The one that we find helpful is the one developed by Brown and Lamont over a number of years and trialled and refined in workshops with clinicians and educators. The protocol is applied to several case studies in SPAA's Ethics Education Package (2002b). The package discusses a series of case studies presenting ethical dilemmas commonly encountered by speech–language pathologists. The ethical reasoning of expert clinicians in response to these case studies is documented in the package. Users are invited to compare their ethical reasoning and outcomes with those provided, recognizing of course that many complex clinical situations and ethical dilemmas have no one answer, or no right answer. The ethical reasoning protocol is outlined in Table 5.5. It has five main stages that involve asking a series of questions, using the prompts provided.

Table 5.5 An ethical reasoning and decision-making protocol

---

1. The facts?
What are the facts and how did you learn about them?
Who is involved?
What are the client-related factors?
What are the external considerations?
Do you need any other facts or information?

2. Is there an ethical problem?
Is there a problem that needs action?
If so, what possible actions are you considering at this early stage of your ethical reasoning?

3. Is there a problem that requires action?
List possible actions that you are considering at the early stage in your ethical reasoning. What are the practical actions and alternatives and likely outcomes?

4. The problem
Which ethical principles apply?
    beneficence (bring about good) and non-maleficence (prevent harm)
    truth
    fairness (justice)
    autonomy
    professional integrity (fidelity)

Which duties, obligations or rules are not being met?
    standards of practice
    laws
    employer's policies
    other professional policies, position papers

What is the conflict? Where is the conflict? (e.g. between principles; between duty versus outcome; between ethics and external factors)

4. Proposed decision and action plan
Make a decision and indicate your action plan

5. Evaluation plan
Consider how you will evaluate and reflect on this process and its outcome

---

Adapted from the Speech Pathology Association of Australia, Ethics Education Package (2002b) with permission.

Developing clinical reasoning: clinical educators and students working together

Professional environments are fraught with ethical dilemmas. The clinical environment provides multiple exemplars of ethically complex cases, which require students and their clinical educators to apply ethical reasoning and reach ethical decisions about management of clients, service provisions, discharge and so on. As work environments and clients become more complex, the need will increase for clinicians as well as students to improve their ethical reasoning and decision-making. Students and clinical educators can support the development of ethical reasoning in each other in two key ways:

1. Taking informal serendipitous opportunities to act as critical companions (Titchen, 2001) for each other, asking each other the sorts of problematizing, searching questions outlined in Learning exercise 5.2, which promote articulation of tacit reasoning processes, and self-reflection and critique of reasoning and decision-making processes and outcomes.
2. By formally making time to work through cases seen in daily clinical practice. Using the ethical decision-making protocol provided above, clinical educators and students could make a commitment regularly to work through one complex case, e.g. once per week. We have found that such case discussion is a useful professional development activity for a whole speech–language pathology department, not just for students and their clinical educators.

Basic ethics education for students

As well as providing students with opportunities to develop their ethical reasoning in relation to client management, students may also need to be educated about the special ethical problems that confront them as students learning to be professionals, e.g. the concept of confidentiality can be difficult for some students to grasp. They may not appreciate reasons why they cannot talk about their fascinating clients with family and friends, especially when they hear their clinical educators doing just this with colleagues in the lunchroom. Students also may not appreciate that talking about their clinical educators with their peers at university can be seen as unethical. Vignette 5.2 illustrates a student struggling with her desire to have her peers help her develop ways of managing her clinical educator while avoiding unethical gossip. As you read this vignette, think about ways in which the student could achieve her goals without behaving unethically.

Vignette 5.2: using peers constructively versus unethical disclosure of information

Cathy was having a difficult time on her placement. Her clinical educator was making what Cathy believed were unrealistic demands of her and rarely offered her positive feedback. Cathy had a strong peer network at university who had worked together for 3 years. They shared clinical resources and hints, and helped each other constructively debrief the challenges and anxieties of clinical placements. Cathy wanted to be able to talk with her peers about her problems with her clinical educator, but was mindful of the lecture that the students had received about ethics in clinical education. She understood that she had a duty to her clinical educator as a colleague to be truthful, respectful, objective and fair. Cathy did not want to be unprofessional and 'gossip' about her clinical educator, but she did want to talk about how upset she felt and seek their advice on ways to manage the situation. Cathy wondered how she might do this in a professional, ethical manner.

Students also face role conflicts peculiar to their status as emerging but not yet qualified professionals, e.g. students may be offered payment for 'doing a quick assessment' or 'providing some exercises' for family members or friends who have communication disorders. They need assistance to understand the legal and ethical pitfalls of responding to such requests.

We have developed some scenarios of possible ethical dilemmas faced by students that we work through with our students. An example of these is provided in Vignette 5.3 below.

Vignette 5.3: ethical dilemmas faced by students

Scenario 1: Mary, an entry level student, is instructed by her clinical educator to telephone the next client on the waiting list and book them in for her next assessment. When Mary consults the waiting list she is dismayed to find that the next client is likely to involve a complex assessment and lots of liaison with other professionals. Mary is concerned that the assessment will be difficult for her and might influence her clinical educator's view of her competency levels. Mary is tempted to skip this client on the waiting list and go on to the next one.

Scenario 2: Judy, a novice student, needs to phone the schoolteacher of her client to discuss the client's performance at school and her current treatment goals. Judy is feeling nervous about making the phone call and is concerned that the teacher will be dismissive of her comments because she is a student. Judy considers whether she will simply omit to tell the teacher that she is a student.

Scenario 3: Josh has been asked by his clinical educator to watch a video of his treatment session and to write a self-evaluation about his performance. Josh takes the video home but, after several days of trying, has been unable to get access to the TV and video when none of his flatmates are present. Josh considers using the TV/video facilities at his local library but again is concerned that someone passing by may recognize the client.

Scenario 4: Sue, an intermediate level student, is asked by a friend to 'take a quick look at my niece, because she is not talking very well'.

Ethical issues in clinical education

Engaging in clinical education may also raise some different ethical issues for clinical educators. Just as clinical educators are required to ensure that ethical behaviour and decision-making occur in relation to clients and services, they are also required to do this in relation to students. Ethically, clinical educators are bound to treat their students with fairness, justice, truthfulness and confidentiality. They are also required to respect the rights of the student to make their own decisions and to prevent harm occurring to them. Vignette 5.4 contains some examples of the types of ethical dilemmas that clinical educators might face and lists the ethical principles that are challenged in each example.

Vignette 5.4: examples of ethical dilemmas faced by clinical educators

Example 1: an ethical dilemma in working with a marginal student
Tanya is currently supervising a student who is struggling to meet the required expectations on placement. Tanya has found that she has needed to spend much more time teaching and facilitating the student's learning, compared with other students she has had in the past. Tanya is aware that the student will be completing her next placement with a different clinical educator in the same organization. Tanya feels that she should warn the next clinical educator that the student may require more time and support, so that the clinical educator can adjust her workload to accommodate this. However, Tanya is also concerned that if she does this then she may be biasing the new clinical educator's initial assessment and view of the student. How can this situation be satisfactorily managed?
Ethical principles to consider: confidentiality, fairness, autonomy, beneficence.

Example 2: ethical challenges in working with racist clients
Carla is currently supervising Jo on clinical placement. Jo is an advanced level speech–language pathology student from an Asian background. Jo has excellent English language skills and a mild accent that does not impair her intelligibility or clinical competence. Carla observes one of Jo's clients making repeated racist remarks to her. She also observes the client making progress towards their treatment goals within the session. Although Jo manages the client within the sessions well, she is visibly upset when the session finishes. Carla wonders how she should manage this situation.
Ethical principles to consider: non-maleficence, autonomy, justice, confidentiality.

Example 3: the ethics of disclosure by students
Daniel, a speech–language pathology student, has bipolar disorder. On his final clinical placement, because he needed to have a few days absent from the placement during a phase of depression, Daniel chose to disclose to his clinical educator that he has bipolar disorder. Daniel wanted his clinical educator to know that his absences from the placement were for a genuine reason and to explain why he appeared withdrawn and tired for the few days before his absence. At the time, Daniel's clinical educator was understanding and supportive, and Daniel received an excellent final assessment from his clinical educator. Some months later Daniel applied for a new graduate position in the same department in which his clinical educator worked and was not granted an interview. Daniel wondered if somehow his disclosure of bipolar disorder had ruined his chances of being considered for the position.
Ethical principles to consider: confidentiality, fairness, justice.

The second example, in particular, illustrates a situation in which the clinical educator needs to make ethical decisions in relation to both the client and the student. The first and third are examples where ethical decisions need to be made in relation to the student and the organization. When these situations arise, clinical educators need access to support and advice from colleagues and/or the university about ways of managing the situation in an ethical manner. Clinical educators also need to be aware that they are providing a powerful role-model for students with regard to ethical behaviour when they make decisions about clients, and sometimes the students themselves. We have met many students who have become cynical and disillusioned about the profession when they observe or experience clinical educators engaging in unethical behaviours.

Conclusion

Ethical reasoning and behaving ethically are a continual challenge for both students and clinical educators. They remain a constant focus of learning in clinical practice. The development of ethical reasoning and clinical reasoning more broadly, along with personal skills needed for professional practice are facilitated by a number of learning processes. These are discussed in the next chapter.

CHAPTER 6
Development of learning processes

This chapter addresses the issue of how students and clinical educators learn through discussion of a range of potential learning processes. The common thread that underpins all of the learning processes presented is reflection. The processes are simply ways of encouraging reflection through different learning approaches or styles.

Throughout this chapter learning processes for students and clinical educators are discussed side by side. For students to become life-long learners it is important that they observe their clinical educators engaging in learning, modelling life-long learning, and discussing and critiquing their learning. We believe that students need to experience and explore a variety of learning approaches throughout their education. Graduates need to know how they learn best, but they also need to be able to learn using any learning process when their preferred learning process is not an option. Also, if clinical educators are truly life-long learners, they will be continually engaged in learning processes.

The focus on reflection in this chapter does not imply that other learning approaches not based on reflection are insignificant. It is still the case that much of the propositional knowledge associated with professional practice can be taught and learned through other methods; however, the next section argues that processes based on reflection are necessary for effective learning within the clinical context.

The importance of reflection

Reflection is the means by which learners can make sense of and integrate new learning into existing knowledge. 'All learning builds on existing perceptions and frameworks of understanding and links must be made between what is new and what already exists if learners are to make sense of what is happening to them' (Boud and Edwards, 1999, p. 175).

Reflection allows learning to occur through the identification and inclusion of individuals' related prior learning, beliefs, values and attitudes.

Clinical practice often involves complex problems, ill-defined goals, unpredictable outcomes and highly individualized prior life experiences of both clients and professionals. No textbook, clinical research trial, published article or commercial programme will ever solve every problem or meet the needs associated with working with individuals, groups of students, groups of clients or groups of professionals in the healthcare context – hence, the need for reflection in clinical practice because it facilitates the integration of propositional knowledge with knowledge about the individual or group and self-knowledge. Boud and Edwards (1999) suggest that reflecting on learning experiences 'accommodates the physical, emotional and intellectual complexities of clinical and fieldwork settings' (pp. 174–175).

The process of reflection will lead to holistic clinical reasoning and decision-making, and ultimately the shift from novice to expert in the area that is being consistently reflected upon. Reflection is a tool that will not only assist clinical reasoning (see Chapter 5) but also facilitate creation and integration of professional practice and personal growth.

Readers are directed to the work of Schön (1983) and Fish and Coles (1998) if they are interested in exploring further the purpose and power of reflection in contemporary clinical practice by health professionals. Reflection can also be used to increase learning by clinical educators in relation to their educational practices. Here is another of the parallels that are drawn throughout this book. Reflection can facilitate the learning of students and clinical educators about clinical practice, as well as the learning of clinical educators about their clinical education practices. Reflection by clinical educators may also help clarify and deepen their sense of self and sense of relationship with others (McAllister, 2001), and thereby support professional development in the role of clinical educator.

The process of reflection

There are several models of the reflection process. Boud et al. (1985) describe a three-stage model of reflection. This model was adapted for speech–language pathology clinical education by Mandy in 1989. Boud and Edwards (1999) proposed a model for promoting learning from experience that also incorporates the three-stage model. The three stages in the model are:

- Stage 1: returning to the experience
- Stage 2: attending to feelings
- Stage 3: re-evaluating the experience.

In stage 1 the learner mentally revisits the learning experience and attempts to recapture, in detail, the events that formed the experience. In stage 2 the learner focuses on the feelings and emotions that were present during the experience. Boud and Edwards (1999) contend that feelings can inhibit or enhance further reflection and learning. Negative feelings have the potential to influence future perceptions or possibly block understanding. Positive feelings may be celebrated and used to increase motivation for further learning.

In stage 3, the learner re-evaluates the experience using the benefit of hindsight and incorporating the insights gained from returning to the experience and attending to the feelings associated with it. Boud and Edwards (1999) propose that there are four aspects to this stage: association, where new information is related to old; integration, where relationships are sought between new and old information; validation, where the authenticity for the learner of the new ideas is tested; and appropriation, where new knowledge is made one's own and incorporated into the learner's knowledge base. Below is Boud and Edwards' (1999) model which also highlights the context or 'social milieu' in which learning occurs (Figure 6.1).

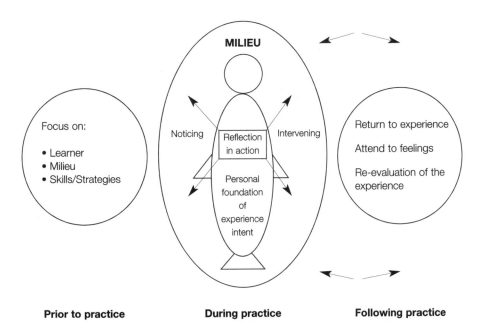

Figure 6.1 Boud and Edwards model. (Reproduced with permission Elsevier Ltd from Educating Beginning Practitioners: Challenges for health professional education by Higgs and Edwards, 1999.)

The model of reflection discussed above is essentially a model of reflection on action (Schön, 1983), in that it occurs after the learning experience. Boud and Edwards' (1999) model also incorporates reflection in action (Schön, 1983) as a way of conceptualizing how learning can occur during a learning experience. Reflection in action involves noticing or observing an event, feeling or reaction, intervening by interpreting what is noticed, and taking action to change the learning milieu (Boud and Edwards, 1999) or the learner. For the most part, reflection in action is invisible. However, in the clinical context, the presence of reflection in action is evident when a series of unproblematic activities and decisions occur. Arguably, for student learners reflection on action would seem to be a prerequisite skill for the development of reflection in action. The development of skills in reflection in action is manifested in the clinical setting by flexibility in the approaches taken, an ability to terminate and change activities, and the ability to seek help or assistance when necessary. Many clinical educators will reflect both on and in action about their clinical work; however, novice clinical educators may begin reflecting about their work as clinical educators after placements or after supervisory interactions with students. We believe that clinical educators who demonstrate the ability to reflect in action during interactions with students are demonstrating the 'artistry' of their work.

Reflection for students

It is likely that most students spontaneously reflect in an unplanned, unconscious manner (Lincoln et al., 1997b). Many of the requirements for students demand that some level of reflection occurs, e.g. by requiring session or lesson plans from speech–language pathology students we require them to revisit what occurred in the previous lesson and engage in forward planning from that point. Students can be encouraged to engage in planned and deliberate reflection as a means of facilitating their learning (Table 6.1). Planned reflection results in aware and conscious decision-making. It allows knowledge of the clinical reasoning process along with accurate decision-making.

Table 6.1 Student learning activities that require reflection

Producing treatment plans
Report and progress note writing
Self-assessment
Supervisory conferencing
Log book recording
Journalling
Writing/reporting critical incidents

Reflection for clinical educators

Fish and Coles (1998), in their book, report that 'sadly most professionals do not have opportunity in the course of their daily practice to look in depth at what they do routinely and resolve its complexity' and that this leaves a 'gap in their professional lives of never clearly understanding the basis of one's professional practice' (p. 2). Further to this, both Fish and Coles (1998) and Trede (2000) believe that professional 'artistry' is a result of reflection. Trede (2000) defines artistry as treating patients as individuals and making use of personal knowledge and past experiences to add an intuitive quality to clinical expertise. It is likely that some of the tasks that speech pathologists regularly engage in facilitate reflection; however, the depth and time given to that reflection are no doubt influenced by the pressures experienced in contemporary clinical practice. Some tasks that may potentially facilitate reflection are presented in Table 6.2.

Table 6.2 Speech–language pathologists' tasks that may facilitate reflection

Considering ethical issues
Report and progress note writing
Statistics collation
Team meetings
Case presentations
Programme planning
Quality assurance activities
Service reviews

Speech–language pathologists who are also clinical educators will benefit from reflection on their experiences during clinical education placements. The interpersonal relationships that exist in the triad of student, client and educator (Maloney and Sheard, 1992) are likely to provide much material worthy of planned and conscious reflection. In addition, the education of students requires the identification and implementation of careful and considered strategies for facilitating student learning. Again, the complexity and challenge of this task are increased by the individuality of the interactants. Reflection is also a means by which professional artistry in clinical education can be developed.

Ways of facilitating reflection

As discussed above, both students and clinical educators routinely perform tasks that require them to engage in some reflection. In the best-case scenario, the tasks may be the catalyst for planned in-depth reflection, and in the worse-case scenario the tasks may prompt superficial, cursory reflection. The following is a discussion of other factors that may facilitate reflection for students and clinical educators.

Students require a time and place to reflect. The provision and acknowledgement of reflection time during a busy clinical placement will underscore for students the importance of reflection in their professional learning and growth. Similarly, if possible, students should be provided with a space in the clinic where they can be alone or can talk confidentially with their peers or clinical educators. Besides physical considerations, students are more likely to engage in reflection if the clinical environment is one in which staff members model reflection both in and on action, and learning processes are actively discussed. This of course is predicated on the assumption that clinical educators are able to allocate time for reflection.

Clinical educators require time away from students to allow them to engage in reflection about the supervisory relationship and process in which they are engaged. 'Sharing' students with other staff members or having designated 'time-out' periods across a week can help clinical educators organize time away from students. Similarly, workplace managers can support reflective practice by scheduling and valuing debriefing and problem-solving discussions with colleagues about clinical education issues. Universities can also play a role in this area, by providing workshops and seminars that facilitate learning through reflection on prior clinical education experiences.

Choosing reflective learning processes

As stated earlier, we believe that students need the opportunity to explore and use a variety of learning processes. By doing this they will be able to identify which approaches suit their learning style best, which are the most effective for them, and with which they feel the most comfortable and least resistant. We also recognize that learners do not always have the freedom to choose how they will learn new material, e.g. information about a new treatment technique may be available only through attendance at a workshop. This may not be an ideal learning situation for learners who prefer to learn through reading and experimentation. Consequently, exposure to and critique of a variety of learning processes are an important part of the educational process.

Self-evaluation

'Self-evaluation is a learning process in which individuals set goals and evaluate their progress towards these goals, but are not ultimately

responsible for producing grades or marks about their performance'
(Lincoln et al., 1997a,b). Speech–language pathology students are often
required to self-evaluate as part of their clinical education experiences
(Kenny, 1996). The aim of self-evaluation is to foster the development of
'self-supervision' (Dowling, 2001). In other words, self-evaluation should
lead to the ability to evaluate performance, monitor progress, diagnose
learning needs and set meaningful learning goals. Boud (1989) believes
that 'the need to monitor one's own performance is one of the defining
characteristics of professional work' (p. 21). Taken together, the work of
Boud and Kenny suggests that self-evaluation is a critical learning process
for both students and practitioners. Table 6.3 lists ways that students,
practitioners and clinical educators may engage in self-evaluation.
Appendix 6.1 at the end of the chapter contains a list of prompts that may
assist learners in the self-evaluation process.

Table 6.3 Self-evaluation strategies

Strategy	Explanation
1. Watching videos of clinical sessions or supervisory conferences	Facilitates reflection by helping the learner return to the event and recall what happened in detail and perhaps re-experience the emotions associated with it
2. Written self-evaluation	The learner follows through on the three stages of the reflective process (i.e. returning to the experience, attending to the feelings, re-evaluating the experience) by writing about each one and then reflects further on the learning goals they have set and how they are being achieved
3. Supervisory conferences	Supervisory conferences can occur in which the specific aim of the discussion is to facilitate reflection (Kenny, 1996). The facilitator attempts to be non-directive during the interaction and aims to respond to the level of awareness of insight achieved by the learner rather than the accuracy of their recounting of events
4. Case presentation	Preparing for and conducting a case presentation requires the learner to integrate the current state of his or her knowledge and reflect on the decisions and outcomes
5. Data-based self-evaluation	Learners may use counting and tallying methods to assist them to self-evaluate their progress towards goals, e.g. students may tally the number of times they gave specific versus non-specific feedback during a treatment session (Culatta and Seltzer, 1977; Horton and Byng, 2000; Ferguson and Elliot, 2001)

Journalling

Journal writing is also a learning process that facilitates reflection. Journal writing is not used 'primarily to communicate with others, but rather it orders and represents one's own learning and thinking' (Stockhausen and Creedy, 1994, p. 77). One of the benefits of journal writing is that it slows down thinking as the writer physically constructs words and sentences, and in doing so allows space and time for insight, reorganization of thoughts and revelations. Another benefit of journalling is that it allows the expression and acknowledgement of both positive and negative emotions. This in turn will assist with the reflection process by allowing the learner to move beyond the emotions and begin to re-evaluate the experience.

Beginning level speech–language pathology students at the University of Sydney are required to keep a journal about their first clinical experiences. The journals are submitted mid-way through the semester and are checked to ensure that students are engaging in the three stages of the reflective process. We have observed a tendency, over the years, for some students simply to recall the events of clinical sessions without progression to attending to feelings and re-evaluating the experience. However, with direction and prompting students are able to engage fully in the reflective process via their journals. Students demonstrate emerging abilities in synthesizing information, applying and evaluating theory, and unearthing personal values and beliefs in their journal writing. The following are extracts from novice students' journals.

Vignette 6.1: examples of students' journal entries

Example 1: returning to the experience
We sat on the floor and played with the doll's house and I wrote down a language sample as we played. It was difficult to write and play at the same time.

Example 2: attending to feelings
I was glad that I had the tape recorder on and I felt bad that I wasn't giving John all of my attention; he seemed to sense that I wasn't fully engaged in the task and quickly became bored and started looking for something else to do.

Example 3: re-evaluating the experience
Next time I will try to video-record the language sample so I can give the client my full attention and perhaps have thought of some interesting things to do with the toys so I can make the interaction a bit more interesting for the client.

raises a number of issues that must be considered
arizes these issues.

...der when using journals

	Options
1. _____ e	As close to the time of the experience as possible (Holly, 1987). When the learner feels a need to write or at home afterwards when pressures are removed (Lincoln et al., 1997b)
2. Whether to provide structure or not	Novice journal writers may benefit from being provided with a structure to prompt their writing. Writing that is for a specific purpose or is focused on a particular issue may be facilitated by the provision of some structure. Appendix 6.2 contains prompts to help learners write structured journals
3. Confidentiality	When encouraging or requiring students to write journals it should be explicit from the start whether they will be required to allow others to read their journals. Alternatively students may be allowed to submit extracts from journals, indicate sections of their journals that they do not want read by others or provide a verbal summary of the material contained in their journal
4. Commenting on journal writing	Journals are personal writing so any comments about the content of journals needs to be approached with this in mind. Evaluative or judgemental statements should be avoided. Affirming statements or questions are more likely to facilitate deeper reflection
5. Assessing journals	It is difficult to assign a grade or mark to journals, because this would require judgements about degree of reflection and insight. Our preference is for journals to be a requirement of a course rather than a graded piece of work
6. Sharing journals	Colleagues, peers, clinical educators and students may share their journals with each other as a way of communicating about their experiences. Thoughtful and constructive feedback to another via commenting on their journal entries is a way of facilitating reflective learning
7. Self-disclosure in journalling	The degree of self-disclosure in journals will reflect the personality of the student and also the intended audience. Assessable journals and journals that are read by people in authority are less likely to contain self-disclosure than those that will be read by peers. Self-disclosure in journals should be treated in a confidential manner

As discussed in Table 6.4, clinical educators may also write a journal to facilitate their own learning. This learning process may be particularly helpful for people who enjoy writing or those who feel a need to 'slow down' their thought processes. Stockhausen and Creedy (1974) describe the practice of students and clinical educators sharing excerpts from their journals at a weekly meeting. The reciprocal nature of this practice serves both to model and to affirm reflective practice.

Peer learning

The third learning process that is discussed here is peer learning. It is likely that this is one of the most common learning processes used by clinical educators. Informal discussions in hallways and staff rooms, as well as more formal case presentations, lectures and workshops run by colleagues, are all examples of opportunities for peer learning. Students can also learn from their peers in a similar manner, e.g. though discussion, observation of each other's clinical sessions and through semi-formal presentations. Table 6.5 compares peer learning opportunities for students and clinical educators.

Table 6.5 Opportunities for peer learning

Opportunities for clinical educators	Comparable opportunities for students
Informal discussion	Informal discussion
Case presentation	Case presentation to other students
Interest groups	Specialist placements for students with similar interests
Lectures	Presentations by peers
Workshops	Workshops by peers
Observation of clinical work	Observation of clinical work
Departmental meetings	Supervisory conferencing with other students (see Farmer and Farmer, 1989)
Working parties	Group assignments
Journal clubs	Group assignments

The main difference here for clinical educators and students is their respective peer groups. By definition a peer is someone of equal or similar standing, and consequently the opportunities for learning from fellow students will be somewhat different to the opportunities for learning from one's professional peers. However, regardless of the peer group, reflection can occur as part of peer learning. Through discussion with peers, students or clinical educators can be encouraged to return to an experience and identify the feelings associated with it, i.e. recount what happened and how they felt, and then re-evaluate the experience. Perhaps reflection with peers is more likely to result in honest identification of feelings compared with self-evaluating with a manager or, for students, self-evaluating with a clinical educator.

Ways of facilitating peer learning

As with journalling and self-evaluation, allowing time for engaging in peer learning is critical for both clinical educators and students. Vignette 6.2 is a brief account of peer learning by clinical educators

Vignette 6.2: peer learning by clinical educators

Mary had just given her student a mid-placement assessment. The student had challenged the grades that Mary had assigned to a number of skills, complaining that Mary had no evidence to support the grades she had given. Eventually Mary left the discussion feeling angry and frustrated. Fortunately Sally her colleague was in the office next door and Mary decided to 'let off steam' about the student with Sally. Sally listened while Mary described the interaction with the student and, with Sally's prompting, labelled in detail her feelings throughout the discussion, e.g. at one stage she had felt threatened by the student's insistence that she did not have evidence for the grades she had assigned; at another time she felt helpless because the student appeared to have no insight regarding his own behaviour and yet at another stage she felt pleased that the student had progressed well in a particular skill area. Through this process Mary came to the conclusion that she needed to keep more detailed records of the student's learning experiences and to keep copies of all the written feedback she provided to him, so that she would have more evidence to support her grades next time. Mary also decided to discuss some possible learning experiences with the student that would help develop his self-evaluation skills. Through discussion with her peer Sally, Mary was able to return to the event, discharge her negative feelings, learn from the experience and formulate new goals for herself in the supervisory process.

Students may require both structured and unstructured approaches to facilitating peer learning (Lincoln and McAllister, 1993). Examples of unstructured facilitatory techniques are the provision of two or more students at placement sites, the provision of observation facilities and modelling of peer learning by clinical educators. Examples of more formal approaches to facilitating peer learning are case presentation, peer tutoring and supervisory conferences. Clinical educators may conduct group supervisory conferences with all students on placement to encourage the exchange of information and ideas. Another possibility is workplace or university-based training in facilitating others' learning.

Titchen (1998) describes a facilitative learning relationship between an experienced and a less experienced peer as 'critical companionship'. The more experienced peer provides constructive criticism and support and acts as a resource for the less experienced peer. The experienced peer through careful and thoughtful questioning may assist his or her peer to move through the three stages of reflection and to achieve a higher level of integration of knowledge as a result (see Chapter 4).

Feedback

Providing students with feedback about their clinical performance is one of the primary tasks of clinical educators. Clinical educators use feedback to students to facilitate learning. Similarly, students can give feedback to clinical educators about their skills in clinical education, and this information can be used by clinical educators to facilitate their learning. Once again feedback can be aimed at facilitating reflection. It can help direct the learner to return to a particular experience and begin the process of re-evaluating and learning from the experience. Vignette 6.3 gives examples of feedback that clinical educators have written to students.

Vignette 6.3: examples of feedback to students

Example 1
When the client squealed in delight during the game, I noticed that a look of concern crossed your face; I wonder what disturbed you about this incident?

Example 2
Do you think you would do this activity the same way again next time? How might you change it to meet your goals for the client better?

Example 3
When the client began to cry, you managed this well by appearing to remain calm and giving them time to compose themselves.

All three examples of written feedback above are deliberate statements designed to encourage reflection by students on their clinical interactions. The three examples in Vignette 6.4 are feedback that students have written to clinical educators.

Vignette 6.4: examples of feedback to clinical educators

Example 1
It helps me to learn when you give specific examples of things that I didn't do quite right.

Example 2
I find it hard to generate answers to your questions on the spot but I can come up with answers if you give me some more time.

Example 3
Watching you present an in-service to the teaching staff was the best learning experience I have ever had!

Similarly the three examples in Vignette 6.4 would facilitate reflection by clinical educators on the learning strategies they use in the clinical education process.

Feedback can be given either in writing or verbally and it may be elicited in a structured or an unstructured way. A clinical educator may elicit verbal feedback in an unstructured manner by simply asking the student how his or her placement is going. They may also choose to elicit feedback by asking a student to complete a written questionnaire about their experiences. Clinical educators provide structured written feedback to students by completing their clinical assessments (see Chapter 7). Ideally students will be well prepared for the assessment results through the provision of less formal feedback throughout the placement. We believe that reciprocity of feedback is a powerful tool to assist in redressing the power differential inherent in every clinical educator/student relationship (McLeod, 1989). It also reinforces and provides a tangible illustration of life-long learning at work in clinical education and practice.

Accepting and acting on feedback

It is important to establish boundaries before clinical educators or students begin giving feedback (Lincoln et al., 1997a). The establishment of boundaries provides a safe and supportive context within which learning will occur. We have found that drawing a boundary around the student–client–clinical educator relationship is helpful for students. The clinical educator informs the student that all material, events and student experiences relating to client management are within the boundaries of the feedback process. Other issues, e.g. personal issues, are outside those boundaries. However, when personal issues are influential within the boundaries of the student–client–clinical educator relationship, feedback will be given on these issues.

Accepting negative and sometimes positive feedback can be a challenge for both students and clinical educators. The acceptability of feedback can be increased by adhering to some of the guidelines for giving feedback presented in Table 6.6.

Table 6.6 Guidelines for giving feedback

Focus feedback on the impact of behaviours on clients
Avoid emotional or heavily connoted language
Give a balance of both positive and negative feedback
Be specific, give examples
Use data collection to support your observations
Suggest possible options or alternative approaches to problems
Pose questions that will facilitate learning

Clinical educators can work with students to improve their ability to accept negative feedback if necessary. In our experience, helping students understand the intention of the feedback, along with helping them identify their own emotional responses to feedback, can be helpful. Typically students may have a defensive response to negative feedback that is unhelpful from a learning point of view. Assisting students to identify when they are feeling defensive and discussing and practising ways of responding non-defensively can be helpful. Of course one of the most powerful learning experiences for students is watching clinical educators accept feedback from students, peers or managers in a non-defensive manner.

Along with giving feedback there is an expectation that change and growth will occur. If the intention of giving feedback is to facilitate learning, it is reasonable that both clinical educators and students will expect change from the recipient of the feedback. It is our belief that clinical educators should not ask students for feedback about their clinical education skills unless they are prepared to act on the feedback and are open to change.

Conclusion

This chapter has described several learning processes that both students and clinical educators can utilise to facilitate reflection on clinical practice and clinical education experiences. It has stressed the importance of students experiencing a variety of learning processes. We have emphasised that one potential educational objective for speech–language pathology students is to develop the ability to learn via any learning process. This chapter has also discussed numerous ways that speech–language pathologists can continue to learn about their own clinical and clinical education practices.

Appendix 6.1: Prompts to assist learners when self-evaluating

- What was your overall impression of the session?
- What things went well during the session and what did you learn from these?
- What things went wrong during the session and what did you learn from these?
- What emotions can you remember feeling during the session?
- Did you observe or think about client emotions or behaviours during the session?
- Did you observe or think about any of your own emotions or behaviours during the session?
- Did the session follow your plan? Why or why not?
- What theoretical knowledge did you use or could you have used during this session?
- What past experiences did you use or could you have used during this session?
- What do you need to learn or find out about before the next session?

Appendix 6.2 Prompts to assist students to write structured journals (adapted from Smith, 1987)

- Brief description of the clinical experience
- The participants, the sequence of events, what you did
- Important observations you made about the clinical experience
- The client's behaviour, your behaviour, what others observed
- What you learned from the experience
- Was this consistent with your theoretical knowledge and prior experience?
- What would you like to change for next time?
- Be specific – behaviours, activities, procedures, participants
- How will you change these?

Identify how you will measure these changes.

CHAPTER 7

The art of learning from assessment

Assessment involves appraisal of individuals' current levels of performance or achievement relative to a set of defined standards or performance criteria. The focus of assessment is usually on collecting, analysing and reporting information on what the person can do (Smith, 2001). The task of formally assessing students to meet university requirements is perhaps one of the most anxiety-provoking activities in which clinical educators and students engage. In general, clinical educators are concerned about providing students with valid and fair assessments, and students are concerned about performing to the best of their ability and being fairly assessed. This chapter addresses issues surrounding the validity and fairness of assessment and discusses ways of promoting learning through valid and fair assessment. The chapter focuses on the clinical assessment of students and the assessment of clinical educators. Whether we like it or not, students, colleagues and universities will assess and report either formally or informally on the skill level of clinical educators. Ways of eliciting assessment from others and learning from their assessment are discussed in this chapter.

Setting the scene for a discussion of assessment

Before launching into a discussion of methods of assessment and ways to facilitate learning from assessment it is important to consider two issues first: the purpose of assessment and the impact of assessment on students' learning. According to Robertson et al. (1997) there are multiple reasons for assessing students. Table 7.1 presents an adaptation of their original list of seven reasons for assessing. The list has been adapted to broaden the focus from health science students to learners in general.

Table 7.1 Reasons for assessing learners

To detect mastery
To increase the motivation of learners
To identify learning needs
To identify teaching needs
To facilitate further learning
To predict an individual's potential
To provide evidence of competence or emerging competence
To compare students' performance to established standards or criteria
For accreditation (to meet the requirements of an external organization)
For comparison with other learners

Table 7.1 highlights that both assessors and assessees need to be aware of the purpose each time that they engage in the assessment process, e.g. assessment of speech–language pathology students at the point of graduation is for the purpose of detecting mastery, for accreditation, for comparison with others and to identify future learning needs. Mid-placement assessment of less experienced students may be for the purpose of increasing motivation, identifying learning needs, identifying teaching needs and predicting individuals' potentials. Students' assessments of clinical educators at the conclusion of placements may fulfil some of the following purposes: to identify learning needs, to facilitate further learning and to provide evidence of competence (to themselves, to the university or to managers). Given the multiple purposes of assessment it is not surprising that it is a complex and challenging activity.

'Assessment drives learning . . . it tells us what to learn' (Boud, 2000). Hence the content and process of assessment will shape what and how learners learn. It is important to keep this in mind throughout this chapter; as educators we must continually ask ourselves what influences our assessment practices are having on our students' learning. We can be certain that our students are asking themselves: what do I need to learn to pass the assessment? To achieve the goals of clinical education, as discussed in Chapter 1, our assessment techniques need to facilitate preparation for complex and changing work environments, the development of generic attributes, the facilitation of life-long learning and the development of social responsibility and cross-cultural competence. How can we meet some of the purposes of assessment outlined in Table 7.1 as well as achieve the outcomes stated above? A partial answer to this question is to facilitate and develop the assessment skills of our students, so that they can accurately identify their own learning needs and continually assess their progress towards their learning goals. By doing this we will also be facilitating students' abilities to assess their peers and clinical educators accurately and fairly.

Some terminology

The literature on assessment contains some key terminology that requires clarification at the outset.

Formative versus summative assessment

Formative assessment can be viewed as part of the feedback process (Stengelhofen, 1993) (see Chapter 6). It is designed to be developmental and facilitative of learning. One of the key aspects of formative assessment is that students have the opportunity to use the feedback and produce an improved performance (Boud, 2000). Formative assessment gives learners information about their current level of performance and ways to improve that performance, e.g. if a clinical educator receives feedback from her students that they are not being challenged enough in their clinical experiences, the clinical educator can reassess the types of experiences that she is providing and take steps to increase the complexity of clients with whom students are involved. A period of formative assessment generally precedes summative assessment.

Summative assessment is the formal appraisal of various aspects of performance. It usually involves the assigning of numerical values to those aspects (Robertson et al., 1997). In a nutshell, summative assessment may be viewed as making a record of learners' current levels of performance. We believe that summative assessment should both celebrate learners' achievements and direct their attention towards the next set of skills, knowledge, attitudes or attributes that they need to focus on developing.

Continuous and end-point assessment

Clinical education placements are the ideal venue for continuous assessment. Clinical educators are able to observe and assess students' performance across clients, contexts and time. Multiple examples of behaviours can be used to assess performance. End-point assessment refers to assessment at a particular time or stage of a course, subject or placement, e.g. students may receive an end-point assessment at the end of a placement. This assessment is likely to be summative in that it records the levels of performance that students achieved by the end of their placement. Students' assessment of clinical educators' performance can also be both continuous and end-point. It is likely that, throughout placements, students are continually assessing the quality of the teaching that they receive. Many clinics and universities also invite or require students to submit an end-point assessment of themselves and their clinical educators at the conclusion of the placement.

Competency-based assessment and generic attributes

Competency-based assessment is the assessment of a person's competence against prescribed standards (Gonczi et al., 1993). In general terms, the assessment usually involves matching students' performances to a detailed set of competencies. In Australia, the Speech Pathology Association of Australia (SPAA) has developed Competency-Based Occupational Standards for Speech Pathologists (CBOS – SPAA, 2001), which lists the competencies that can be expected from 'entry level speech pathologists'. Each university speech pathology degree programme must demonstrate that its assessments allow for determination of whether graduates have met the specified competencies, before graduates from that university can be considered as eligible for membership of the professional association. Appendix 7.1 contains extracts from CBOS (SPAA, 2001). Many Australian universities have incorporated CBOS into their clinical assessment tools, which has made the relationship between the goals of clinical education experiences and professional entry standards transparent.

One of the criticisms of competency-based assessment is that it can potentially fail to capture the generic attributes necessary for effective clinical practice. Generic attributes such as ethical and moral decision-making, professional behaviour towards clients and colleagues, critical thinking abilities and holistic management of clients are the hallmarks of professionalism. Robertson et al. (1997) report that these generic attributes are often the area in which marginal students experience the greatest difficulty. Generic competencies tend to influence performance across a range of specific competencies, e.g. students experiencing difficulties with time management may perform poorly on competencies relating to timely submission of paperwork, preparation for clinical work, liaison with other professionals, holistic client management and possibly even self-evaluation. One way of addressing this problem is to develop tools that assess generic attributes as well as discipline-specific competencies. A consortium of Australian universities and the SPAA are currently engaged in a large, national, funded research project to develop a valid and reliable tool for the assessment of competency in speech–language pathology students that addresses both aspects of competent clinical performance (Lincoln et al., 2003).

Self-assessment

Self-assessment is about measuring one's own performance against defined standards or criteria. Boud (2000) makes a very strong case for the ability to self-assess being a necessary component of life-long learning. The ability to identify your own learning needs and to assess how well you are meeting those needs falls within the practices of a life-long learner.

Students

From an educational point of view, it would seem that self-assessment must be an integral part of the clinical education process, if life-long learning and the attainment of professional mastery are desired outcomes of the process. Self-assessment is also an example of facilitated and directed

Table 7.2 Student self-assessment

Questions	Ideas
1. What resources are necessary to support student self-assessment?	*Materials* – clearly identified learning objectives or learning outcomes to which students can compare their performance *Facilities* – access to video or audio equipment for recording clinical interactions so they can be reviewed later *Teaching* – specific and consistent feedback on performance from the clinical educator as well as objective, evidence-based feedback on their self-assessments
2. How do we get students to self-assess?	Students can assess themselves using either the same assessment techniques that clinical educators use to assess them, or a different set of materials. In either case the objectives and criteria used by students and clinical educators need to be identical to facilitate realistic setting of learning goals
3. What if the clinical educator does not agree with students' self-assessments?	Falchikov and Boud (1989) suggest that advanced students are more accurate self-assessors than beginning students. Hence the ability to self-assess accurately needs to be facilitated. In our experience beginning level students are caught between feelings of a need to be humble versus unrealistic or inaccurate expectations resulting from a lack of experience. Formative self-assessment experiences can be used to facilitate accurate and insightful self-assessment in preparation for summative self-assessment
4. How much 'weight' should self-assessment carry in the assessment process?	Ideally, clinical educator assessment and self-assessment should be combined to produce a single assessment at the end of placements. This, however, is possible only if both parties agree that the other's assessment is accurate. The collection of evidence over time to support assessment decisions is crucial. Students and clinical educators need to be able to cite examples (and if possible provide copies of reports, notes, written feedback, etc.) that support the proposed assessment result

reflection (see Chapter 4) that targets the development of self-knowledge and personal and professional growth. Table 7.2 lists some potential questions that may arise for clinical educators about student self-assessment and ideas for exploring responses to the questions (also see Vignette 7.1).

There are, of course, limits to student self-assessment. University staff and clinical educators are bound by professional codes of ethics as well as their legal responsibilities to judge students' professional competence and fitness to practise. Ultimately, it is the university staff who decide when students have reached the specified criteria and are judged fit to practice. At this point there is little room for the inclusion of self-assessment, except perhaps as a criterion relating to competency, e.g. 'competently self-assesses own performance'. It would seem logical always to include self-assessment as part of formative assessment practices. However, it remains a challenge to include self-assessment as a valid component of summative assessment.

Vignette 7.1: discrepancies between clinical educator assessment and student self-assessment

Linda was supervising an intermediate level student. During the mid-placement assessment conference Linda reviewed the student's self-assessment of her performance so far. Linda was surprised to note that the student had rated her skills much lower than Linda had. Linda wondered why this might have occurred: was her feedback to the student more negative than she had intended? Did the student have unrealistic expectations about her performance at this level? Was the student afraid to give higher ratings in case Linda might think she was over-confident or conceited? Was the student less competent than she appeared?

Clinical educators

The purpose of self-assessment is markedly different for students and clinical educators. Students are self-assessing as part of a required assessment activity, which is aimed at judging competency for the purpose of meeting criteria that make them eligible to graduate. Clinical educators rarely self-assess in order to meet external, defined criteria. This is likely to occur only if they are completing postgraduate study in clinical education or addressing continuing professional education requirements. Clinical educators are most likely to engage in self-assessment for the purpose of facilitating personal and professional growth, and developing professional artistry in clinical education. McAllister's (2001) model of the experience of being a clinical educator (see Chapter 1) emphasizes reflection and introspection as tools for developing in the role of clinical educator. Self-assessment adds to this process by providing feedback about progression towards professional artistry and will aid in the development of new learning goals that extend development further. Table 7.3 considers some potential questions about self-assessment by clinical educators and ideas to consider when formulating answers to the questions.

Table 7.3 Self-assessment for clinical educators

Questions	Ideas
1. How can I self-assess?	It is possible to self-assess in relation to published 'competencies' for clinical education. Several research publications list attributes of clinical educators that students have identified as being helpful to their learning (see Chapter 3). The American Speech–Language–Hearing Association has published competencies for clinical supervision (ASHA, 1982a,b) It is also possible to self-assess relative to prior learning goals, which were identified at the beginning of the placement. This form of self-assessment is highly individualized and embedded within a framework of life-long learning and self-directed professional development
2. What if students do not agree with my self-assessment?	Differing views about the competency of clinical educators most probably arise when students or clinical educators are experiencing failure. It is difficult for people to see clearly while in the midst of a stressful experience. Students and clinical educators may want to blame, rationalize or defend their apparent failure. In this situation other forms of assessment may be more helpful to the learner, e.g. peer assessment. In our experience, accurate self-assessment is more likely to be achieved retrospectively

Vignette 7.2 contains an example of a clinical educator who has identified learning goals for her students before the start of their placement. She has carefully designed learning activities to facilitate achievement of the goals; however, she is unsure how to self-assess whether she has achieved her goals.

Vignette 7.2: determining if you have achieved your goals

At the beginning of her student placements Di decided that she wanted to develop her clinical education skills in the area of helping students identify their attitudes towards elderly patients, and developing awareness about how these attitudes may impact on their ethical decision-making processes. Di developed several learning activities designed to put students in contact with both well and unwell elderly people. She provided discussion time for looking at the needs and rights of elderly patients and finally encouraged students to uncover and articulate their attitudes to elderly people. Di wondered how she would know if she had achieved her goal.

Learning exercise 7.1: self-assessment by clinical educators

Think of ways in which Di could self-assess whether she has achieved her learning goals for the students. Make sure the assessment techniques measure Di's success as a clinical educator, not the success of her students.

Providing formative feedback and assessing progress together

The major purpose of formative assessment is to identify mastery and to set further learning goals. For students and clinical educators formative assessment may also lead to the need to re-negotiate the supervisory process. As new goals are identified, different supervisory strategies will be required to assist students to meet those goals. Consequently new goals are developed simultaneously for students and clinical educators. Vignette 7.3 gives two examples of how a student's and a clinical educator's goals dovetail to facilitate learning by both parties

Vignette 7.3: examples of congruent student and clinical educator goals

Example 1
Student's goal
To increase my independence in clinical reasoning with this caseload.

Clinical educator's goal
• To provide the student with progressively more difficult cases to reason about.

- To hold back from providing the answers to clinical problems in supervisory conferences.
- To structure consistently the questions that I ask the student, to facilitate clinical reasoning.

Example 2
Student's goal
To become more assertive in my interactions with clients and other professionals.

Clinical educator's goal
- To increase my observation of and feedback about the student's interpersonal skills during clinical interactions.
- To provide increased opportunities for the student to practise assertiveness skills.
- To use supervisory conferences to give the student on-line feedback about the appropriateness of their level of assertiveness.
- To model appropriately assertive behaviour with clients and colleagues.

Formative assessment of clinical educators also provides an opportunity for clinical educators to adjust their practices during placements. Clinical educators may ask students to provide written or verbal feedback regarding their clinical education experiences part way through a placement. Students will sometimes identify that the level of supervision that they are given does not match their level of competency. The students may feel they are being over- or under-supervised. We have found that asking students to mark where they feel their skills are on the continuum of supervision (Anderson, 1988) (see Chapter 1), and at what level they feel that they are being supervised, is useful in identifying mismatches between supervisory needs and practices. This approach may help facilitate both students' and clinical educators' moves towards dynamic self-congruence through heightened self-awareness (see Chapter 3).

Formal summative student assessment

The type of formal assessment that students and clinical educators are required to engage in is determined by the university programme. However, sometimes students and clinical educators can decide how the assessment will be conducted and they can usually decide when, where and how the assessment results will be discussed.

It is desirable, for the reasons mentioned above, that student self-assessment be included in formal summative assessment. Table 7.4 describes some possible ways of doing this.

Table 7.4 Ways of including student self-assessment in summative assessment

1. Student and clinical educator complete the assessment individually then meet and compare the assessments. Negotiation occurs over points on the assessment where there is disagreement

2. The student completes the assessment and the clinical educator modifies the assessment where they believe there are discrepancies between the student's self-assessment and actual performance

3. The clinical educator completes the assessment and presents it to the student who is then invited to identify any discrepancies in his or her self-assessment and present evidence to support this self-assessment. The clinical educator can then either reject or accept the student's self-assessment

Typically a specific meeting time is made for the purpose of discussing the assessment. The student should be advised well ahead of time whether they are expected to engage in self-assessment during this meeting, so that they can prepare adequately. Ideally, ample, uninterrupted time in a private location should be provided to discuss the results. Both students and clinical educators should bring to the meeting evidence relating to the areas that are assessed, e.g. copies of written supervisory feedback, written reports, progress notes and session plans.

Perhaps the most important thing that students and clinical educators need to bring to the meeting is an open mind and a non-defensive attitude. Both participants need to be open to hearing and considering the other's point of view, and be prepared to accept feedback in a non-defensive manner. The clinical educator may also take the opportunity to ask the student for feedback on their clinical education skills at this time. This provides an excellent opportunity for clinical educators to model how to receive feedback in a professional manner.

Generally, summative assessments are conducted at the end of a clinical placement. Hence the assessment can be used to assist students in identifying learning goals for subsequent placements. A well-conducted assessment discussion should leave students feeling happy and proud of their achievements, aware of their weaknesses and focused on specific areas of practice to address in the next placement. Students and university placement coordinators will find it helpful to have a written record of the discussion when considering future placement options.

Eliciting feedback from students about clinical education experiences

Most clinical educators and university programmes experience the challenge of eliciting honest and thoughtful feedback from students about their clinical education experiences. In our experience students are sometimes reluctant to give forthright feedback about clinics that are external to the university. Students fear that they may offend or anger a clinical educator who at a later stage may be their employer, colleague or assessor. One way of circumventing this fear is to allow feedback to be given anonymously. However, often clinics may accept only one or two students on placements per year and students correctly believe that their feedback is readily identifiable in these circumstances.

Traditionally, students are asked to provide feedback about the placement site and clinical educator at the end of their placement. Students usually complete a standard form with headings such as those listed in Table 7.5 and submit the form to the university and/or the placement site. This form of feedback is unsatisfactory for several reasons:

- It is too late to make changes to improve learning.
- Students do not have to own or take responsibility for the comments that they make.
- The quality of the form will affect the quality and usefulness of the feedback.
- Students are often tired and rushed at the end of placements and may not reflect adequately at this point in time.

Table 7.5 Some suggested areas for obtaining feedback about placements sites or clinical educators

Resourcing of the site
Preparedness of clinical educator and site for the placement
Number and type of learning opportunities
Adequacy of orientation
Appropriateness of workload (client load and paperwork load)
Frequency and appropriateness of feedback
Communication skills of the clinical educator(s)
Timing, validity and fairness of assessment
Were any problems between clinical educator(s) and student(s) identified and addressed?
Suggestions for change
Would you recommend this placement to another student and why?
Overall rating of placement 1–10, poor–outstanding

The use of such forms does, however, allow the university to exercise some form of 'quality control' over external placement sites. Support, training and mentoring can be provided to sites or clinical educators who receive less than optimal feedback. If, after such intervention, sites or clinical educators continue to receive negative evaluations from students, consideration may be given to not using them for placements in the future. This form of evaluation may also assist university staff in planning professional development activities for clinical educators.

There are several possible alternatives to the end-point evaluation discussed above. Clinical educators may choose to elicit written or verbal feedback from students mid-way through their placements or even on a weekly basis. Honest and considered feedback is most likely to be given within the context of a supportive, non-defensive and confidential relationship. Our experience has been that students are very appreciative and supportive of clinical educators' efforts to change their supervisory practices in response to student feedback.

Alternatively, a third person can participate in the feedback process. During the course of a placement, students can be given the opportunity to provide feedback to a member of staff other than their main clinical educator. The third person is then responsible for passing the feedback on to the clinical educator.

We have used focus groups with students who have all completed placements at the same location to elicit feedback about the placement (see Vignette 7.4). It is essential that this occurs with the full knowledge and permission of the clinical educators involved. The advantage of this approach is that it allows students to remain anonymous, and it also allows the group facilitator and the students to get a sense of what the major issues are and which issues are specific to individual students. Following the focus groups, the facilitator carefully prepares a written summary of the major points, both positive and negative, that are raised and presents these to the placement site for discussion. This process leads to learning for the students, group facilitator and placement site.

Vignette 7.4: focus group feedback from students about a clinical placement

A group of students met with the Director of Clinical Education at their university to discuss their clinical education experiences at a local hospital. The students reported:

• The clinical educator on-site was approachable, knowledgeable and very supportive of student learning.

- The clinical educator clearly communicated her expectations and requirements.
- The caseload was excellent in terms of busyness and variety of clients with communication and/or swallowing difficulties.
- The facilities were excellent with regard to space and equipment.
- Students enjoyed working in the team environment, especially interacting with other allied health students who were on placement at the same time.
- Students felt that the paperwork requirements were excessive and inflexible, e.g. same level of detail required in treatment plans at the beginning and end of the placement.
- Students sometimes felt that other allied health staff within the hospital were not aware of the students' and clinical educators' roles and were not welcoming of students.

The Director of Clinical Education passed on this feedback to the placement site and together they brainstormed ways to act on the students' negative feedback. It was decided to trial:

- Introducing a 'mini' session plan form for students to use when planning for familiar clients or client types with whom they had prior experience.
- Students to be allowed to negotiate the form of treatment plans that they would submit at the mid-placement assessment.
- Clinical educator to discuss her role with her colleagues and the roles of students at a team meeting.
- Clinical educator to notify all allied health staff via email when a new group of students were commencing, and to include their names and level of experience in the email.
- Clinical educator to encourage students to use the lunchroom so as to increase informal contacts with allied health staff.

Learning for and from failing students

Students

Students who fail clinical placements can cause considerable worry and anxiety for their clinical educators. Contrary to student fears, we have yet to meet a clinical educator who enjoys failing students. We have, however, met clinical educators who can successfully fail students. These clinical educators are able to maintain student confidence and motivation at the same time as highlighting significant concerns about their performance. The next section discusses how this can be achieved. The essential feature of failing students successfully is that the failure does not come as surprise to students but rather is the logical conclusion to the learning process outlined in Table 7.6.

Table 7.6 A process for preparing a student for possible failure on placement

1. The student is made aware as early as possible that some areas of their performance require improvement to meet expectations for the placement

2. Strategies for the student to improve their performance are identified, discussed, decided upon and documented

3. Regular monitoring of progress towards achievement of satisfactory performance is conducted, so that it is evident to the student and clinical educator whether the student is making progress

4. If the student does not achieve the required level of performance by the end of the placement, the student fails the placement

5. The clinical educator then focuses on the end of placement performance not on memories of early, less competent performance in the placement

After going through this process, failing should not come as a surprise to a student. The clinical educator is able to congratulate students for the progress that they were able to make and provide assistance to students to evaluate the usefulness of the strategies that they employed. This orientation then leads into a discussion of other strategies for the student to try on the next placement. It is also possible that the student may have achieved satisfactory performance in some previously problematic areas but not all. In this case the discussion would motivate and focus the student on what and how these areas could be addressed.

There are of course several other possible outcomes from failing an assessment that could also be considered positive for students. Sensitive assessment and discussion that identify students' personal strengths and weaknesses may facilitate exploration of other career options. Sometimes failing a placement is the catalyst that precipitates students confronting the appropriateness of their career choice. Receiving accurate and sensitive information about strengths and weaknesses may help students identify other career options that may suit their personal resources. By highlighting and reinforcing strengths, clinical educators may be able to maintain students' senses of self and optimism about their future career prospects. Vignette 7.5 contains an example of a student who successfully failed a placement.

Vignette 7.5: successful failure of a clinical placement

A clinical coordinator with whom we have worked recounted this story in a workshop. 'One of the most surprising interactions I have ever had with a student occurred as a result of excellent supervision. Linda presented herself to my office and announced that she was going to fail her clinical placement and that she wanted to repeat the placement the following semester. When I questioned Linda about the reasons for her failure she was able to say clearly that she needed more time to acquire the necessary skills in several key areas of practice. Linda was comfortable with her failure and focused and optimistic about the future.'

Clinical educators

Working with failing students may challenge clinical educators in many ways. It may cause clinical educators to doubt their own skills in clinical education, e.g. they may ask themselves: could I have done more for the student or done things differently? Or could I have identified the problems earlier or been clearer in my expectations? Failing students may also challenge clinical educators' sense of self and sense of relationships with others, e.g. a clinical educator may be concerned about whether a student will continue to like him or her, what their colleagues might think or whether his or her interpersonal skills were adequate to support the student's learning. Failing students may also highlight for clinical educators their own values, beliefs and attitudes, particularly if these were in conflict with those of the student. Vignette 7.6 is an example of such a conflict.

Vignette 7.6: clinical educator's and student's values and attitudes in conflict

Sharynne's student Kate attended her clinic every day from 9am to 5pm. Sharynne often arrived early or finished later if necessary to complete reports or work on projects. Kate, on the other hand, left promptly at 5pm regardless of whether or not her reports were completed. Sharynne became concerned that Kate's written work was not of an adequate standard – reports often contained grammatical errors and results were sometimes interpreted incorrectly. Sharynne was aware that her work ethic was different from Kate's and she regularly reflected on whether this was influencing her assessment of Kate's written work.

In this vignette, Sharynne's dealings with Kate provided an opportunity for her to explore her sense of self, self in relationship and sense of being a clinical educator.

Planned and deliberate reflection by clinical educators is necessary if learning is to occur from the experience of failing students. Student assessment and self-assessment of a clinical educator's performance will provide direction for the further development of artistry and competency in clinical education. Debriefing with colleagues and university staff may also assist in discharging negative emotions associated with the experience and help give perspective to the experience. The work of McAllister (2001) highlights the need for clinical educators to retain optimism and trust in student motivation, and their capacity to learn and grow if they are to avoid burnout in clinical education.

Conclusion

The combination of self-assessment and formative and summative assessment by students should provide clinical educators with direction in terms of areas to focus on in future placements. We maintain that sustained and focused reflection in conjunction with goal setting and goal achievement is the pathway to the development of professional artistry in clinical education.

Similarly by consistently providing the opportunity for students to self-assess and to receive feedback on their self-assessment, during either formative or summative assessment, we are assisting students to develop competency in assessment.

Appendix 7.1

Examples from the Competency-Based Occupational Standards for Speech Pathologists, Entry Level from the Speech Pathology Association of Australia (2001).

Unit 1: assessment of the client

Element 1: interviews and takes case history
Performance criteria

- The client's and/or significant other's description and perception of the communication and/or swallowing difficulty is identified so that the nature of the problem is clarified and its impact established.
- Information required for speech pathology assessment, diagnosis and intervention is elicited by using an appropriate interview process and collection of data.

Element 6: writes report
Performance criteria

- Reports on the results of assessment, diagnosis, prognosis and planning are written in a style tailored to the recipient and in accordance with the service provider's policies and procedures. Consent is obtained from the client or guardian for reports to be sent to any other person or agency.
- Reports are legible and in English, signed and dated and in the format required by the service provider. Qualified interpreters are used to translate and present the report when necessary.

CHAPTER **8**

A continuum of professional development in clinical education

Throughout this book we have argued that participation in clinical education offers professional development for both students and clinical educators. Professional development in clinical education occurs along a continuum from novice student, to novice clinical educator, to professional artist in clinical education. In this chapter we suggest that preparation for participation in the clinical education process should begin at the novice student level. Understanding and expertise in the clinical education process can continue to develop towards professional artistry throughout speech–language pathology careers. This chapter suggests strategies appropriate to each level of professional development on this journey from novice student to professional artist in clinical education.

In several of the chapters in this book we have described how the learning relationship between clinical educators and students can facilitate a range of personal, professional and clinical knowledge and skills. We have argued that self-knowledge, interpersonal and communication skills, clinical reasoning, ethical decision-making, propositional knowledge, professional craft knowledge and clinical skills can all be developed or enhanced in the context of the clinical education learning relationship. Given the value of clinical education in professional development, it is surprising that it is not accorded more status. In this chapter we consider reasons for the low status of clinical education in universities and the profession at large, and suggest some strategies for improving the status and recognition of clinical education and clinical educators themselves.

The continuum of professional development for clinical educators

Lack of preparation for the role of clinical educator is a chronic problem in speech–language pathology (Anderson, 1988; Rose et al., 1999). Lack

157

of availability, problems with geographical or time access to work-shops/programmes, lack of workplace support for attendance, lack of motivation to attend and lack of relevance have all been cited as reasons why clinicians do not participate in preparation for clinical education. These are real issues that need to be addressed by universities, professional associations, workplaces and clinicians. However, preparation for the role of clinical educator can begin while the clinical educators of the future are still students. In fact, it can begin with novice students undertaking their first placement. In this section, we outline some of the goals and strategies that we use in preparing our students to participate in clinical education and to support the clinical education of peers, as well as strategies and goals around which we structure our preparation programmes for clinical educators.

We will discuss a continuum of professional development of clinical educators using the stages of development described in Chapter 4. If you have not already read Chapter 4, return to that now and read the vignettes of:

- Carol (Vignette 4.6): the novice student
- John (Vignette 4.7): the intermediate level student
- Sue (Vignette 4.8): the entry level student
- Jenny (Vignette 4.1): the novice clinical educator
- Emma (Vignette 4.2): the advanced beginner clinical educator
- Robyn (Vignette 4.3): the competent clinical educator
- Ann (Vignette 4.4): the professional artist.

These vignettes highlight the importance in clinical education of personal knowledge and skills, as well as knowledge and skills in clinical practice of our discipline and in clinical education. We have devoted chapters of this book to discussion of the development of personal skills, cognitive skills, management skills, and teaching and assessment skills. Grounded in these discussions, we have developed goals for the clinical education preparation programmes that we run. These are listed in Table 8.1.

Table 8.1 Goals for clinical education preparation programmes

To increase knowledge of educational processes and methods for developing and extending knowledge and skill in speech–language pathology

To develop a heightened awareness of sense of self, sense of relationship, sense of being a clinical educator and sense of agency

To improve monitoring of meta-mood and metacognition

To develop the confidence and capacity to take appropriate action in a range of roles and tasks required of clinical educators

To encourage speech–language pathologists to strive for professional artistry in clinical education

Preparation of novice students for the clinical education process

Our overall goals with novice students are to make them aware of the clinical education process as well as to participate in it, and to begin the process of personal as well as professional development. We seek to achieve these goals by implementing the strategies listed in Table 8.2.

Table 8.2 Strategies for preparing novice students to participate in and learn about clinical education

Educate them about the clinical education process

Give them experiences in group work, e.g. on assignments so that they begin to develop and analyse the skills needed for effective teamwork and heighten their awareness about themselves as they participate in the group

Develop communication skills

Provide them with experience of being in a mentoring relationship, in this first instance with entry level (final year) students

Provide them with experience of peer observation

Develop skills in reflective journalling or critical incident report writing, so that they can undertake some basic self-evaluation of their clinical or teamwork learning

Give them experience in providing feedback to clinical educators

In educating novice students about the clinical education process, we provide them with basic theory of clinical education, including an overview of models of the clinical education process such as those outlined in Chapter 1, and pathways of professional development available to clinical educators such as those outlined in Chapter 1. The emphasis is on where they as novices are right now and where we want them to be at different stages of their degree. We also discuss how models of the clinical education process suggest different styles of interaction between clinical educators and students at different stages of their professional education and development. This information allows students to begin to create visions of their future self as an entry level student and ultimately speech–language pathology graduate. It also prepares them for the continual change in the nature of expectations and consequently supervisory relationships that they will experience throughout their education.

By participating in group work during tutorials, seminars and assessment tasks such as group assignments, students are given the opportunity to practise and develop their communication skills with peers. In this context students learn and practise negotiation and conflict resolution skills as well as the ability to express their opinions and ideas. Students are also encouraged to reflect upon what role they typically take in group interactions, whether they are able to get their opinion heard, and what communication styles of other students they are comfortable or uncomfortable with. Students may also learn to build a measure of resistance to others' stress or they may find that they are susceptible to taking on others' stress.

We also provide them with opportunities to hear the perspectives of others involved in the clinical education process. We have entry level students with whom they may be linked in a mentoring relationship talk of their experiences of professional growth over the course of the degree programme. We may include them in preparation workshops for clinical educators, both to hear clinical educators' stories and to share their own. We also share with them stories, vignettes and case studies such as those in this book to help them appreciate clinical educators' perspectives.

In our clinical education programmes, one of the most crucial relationships a novice student will have is their mentoring relationship with their assigned entry level student. This person will role-model clinical processes, professional behaviours and approaches to clinical learning for them. Their mentor will, under the supervision of their clinical educator, 'teach' them basic skills in clinic administration and client management, and provide some feedback on their initial attempts in both these areas. This behoves the entry level mentor to have solid skills in clinical practice and clinical education, which we discuss in a later section of this chapter. This mentoring relationship gives the novice student someone from whom to get 'the inside story'. In effective and supportive mentoring relationships, novice students can ask questions of and expect support from their student mentor which they may not do with their clinical educator, for fear of being poorly assessed or 'looking stupid'. We started such novice/entry level mentoring relationships almost two decades ago (Rosenthal, 1986) and continue to find them effective teaching and learning tools for students at all levels of professional development as well as for clinical educators.

We encourage our novice students to observe their peers at work in clinical settings, although not at this stage to give feedback to their peers. We also set them on the path to reflective practice by asking them to journal and/or submit critical incident reports based on their reflective journals. These activities aim to make them aware of the clinical education process and potential learning strategies available to them, their personal response to these and their preferred approaches to learning. Early journalling may start to unearth attitudes, beliefs and biases that students were previously unaware of. Vignette 8.1 is an example from a novice student's journal and feedback to her from her clinical educator which was designed to help her identify the origin of the attitude she had expressed.

Vignette 8.1 Extract from novice student's journal with response from clinical educator

Journal entry

At the end of session it was my job to discuss the homework with the mother. I felt really nervous about this but a part of me was annoyed because I spent ages preparing homework activities prior to the session and I know mum works full-time so won't have time to do much of it.

Feedback

I wonder why you have assumed that mum working full-time means she will not make the effort to do the homework. I wonder what your beliefs and attitudes about mothers who work full-time are and where they have come from.

Finally, we ask our novice students to provide feedback to their clinical educators and entry level mentors, using structured feedback forms such as those discussed in Chapter 7, or face to face during or at the conclusion of a placement. A good time to do this is in the context of a discussion of 'how the placement went' at the conclusion of the placement.

Preparation of intermediate students

With intermediate level students, we use most of the same strategies that we use with novice students but expect a higher level of analysis and critique of their experience and role in their learning. We also expect a greater contribution to the professional development of their peers and clinical educators. We ask them to undertake collaborative paired work with clients. This enlarges the pool of knowledge and skills on which they can draw for planning, client management and reporting, and requires that, as well as observing the practice of their peer, they now also critique and provide appropriate feedback to their peer/partner.

We continue with journals, critical incidents and reflective statements, requiring that these show greater depth of critique and insight into both the clinical process and the clinical education process. We hope to see greater insight into their 'agency' in teaching and learning in these contexts. Insight into personal knowledge and skills, as well as professional knowledge and skills, is anticipated. Intermediate level students take a greater role in assessment of their clinical competence, completing a self-evaluation to take to the assessment session with their clinical educator. We hope to see insightful and accurate self-assessment emerging from students at this level. We also ask for written anonymous feedback to their clinical educators, and may on occasion run focus group debriefing sessions to obtain feedback about sites or placements. Some level of analysis of the students' own roles and responsibilities in the clinical education process, as well as evaluation and critique of their clinical educators, is expected. Group debriefings also allow students to share, in a wider forum, the lessons from placements and clients. Table 8.3 summarizes strategies that we may use with intermediate level students.

Table 8.3 Strategies for developing skills in clinical education for use with intermediate level students

---

Peer observation and feedback

Collaborative paired work with clients

Journals and critical incident reports or reflective statements

Self-evaluation

Participation in assessment of clinical competence

Written anonymous feedback to clinical educators about process

Debriefing/analysing 'stories'

Preparation of entry level students

The processes and goals set in place with novice and intermediate level students continue for entry level students, but expectations increase in terms of the range of roles and responsibilities assumed and insight into the clinical education process expected. As mentioned earlier, entry level students undertake peer mentoring of novice students, involving basic clinical skills teaching, and mid- and end-point assessment of the novice students supported by assessments made by the clinical educator. Clinical educators assume ultimate responsibility for these tasks and in fact mentor the entry level students in these roles. Clinical educators give feedback to the entry level students about their performance as educators and assessors. Our goal is that, by the time entry level students graduate, they will already have skills and experience in the clinical education process on which they can build over the years, rather than coming 'cold' to clinical education when asked to take their first student.

Entry level students continue to work with year peers in designing and providing client services; however, now we expect them to provide more critical (but still sensitive) feedback to their peers about their clinical performance. We also expect that entry level students will be able to provide such oral feedback (as opposed to written feedback) to their clinical educators, as requested, or at least at appointed times such as end-point assessment times. Their ability to undertake these roles and tasks is predicated on an expectation that they will continue to engage in reflective practices such as journalling, and use these as the bases for informed insight and feedback.

A major change in expectations of entry level students is that they will drive the clinical education process. If students have a thorough understanding of the developmental nature of the clinical education process and student/clinical educator interaction, they can be expected to initiate supervisory sessions as needed with their clinical educators, set agendas and lead discussion. It is up to them to manage the timing and content of feedback although, should they fail to take that initiative, their clinical educators will do so (and students will be adversely assessed as a result).

We make good use of our entry level students to provide us with feedback on the entire clinical education programme and to provide us with teaching material for the future. In end-of-programme group debriefs or more formal focus group sessions, stories shared give us an insight into the learning and teaching processes, and provide a quality assurance measure for us. Many of the stories shared in such fora have been transformed into case studies and vignettes for workshops, such as those found in this book. Table 8.4 provides a summary of strategies used with entry level students.

Table 8.4 Strategies for preparation of entry level students for clinical education

Peer mentoring of junior/novice students

Clinical skills teaching

Supported assessment of junior/novice students

Peer observation and feedback of year peers

Oral feedback to clinical educators about the process

Self-assessment of clinical competence

Journalling, critical incidents

Debriefing/analysing 'stories'

Managing the timing and content of feedback from clinical educators and peers

Preparation for clinical educators

As experienced clinical educators (see Chapter 1) have commented:

> The most important thing you bring into the job of being a clinical educator is yourself.

The development of self-knowledge and personal skills should be a key component of professional development programmes for clinical educators. In addition, the move into being a clinical educator marks the start of a steep learning curve, as noted in Chapter 3, and can be marked by anxiety, self-doubt and self-focus as new clinical educators seek to 'survive' their early experiences. The goals for preparation of novice clinical educators are to develop awareness of both self and others, to support and reduce anxiety, and to create a sense of being part of a community of learners, as well as to develop or extend knowledge and skills in clinical education that, it is hoped, they will have developed as students.

Professional development of novice clinical educators

Table 8.5 lists strategies that we have successfully used over many years to prepare and support novice clinical educators.

Table 8.5 Strategies for use in the professional development of clinical educators

Provision of introductory workshops that cover basic theory and skills of clinical education

Careful selection of students to match to site and clinical educator

Sharing student placements with more experienced clinical educators

Provision of mentors

Provision of support from the placing university

Provision of resources for clinical education

Promotion of reflective practice as clinical educators

Inclusion in learning communities of clinical educators

Over the years we have developed a structure, content and resources for introductory workshops that use experiential learning approaches to cover many of the topics we have addressed in this book, including those in Table 8.6.

Table 8.6 Content for introductory workshops for clinical educators

Goals of clinical education

Expectations of all stakeholders in the process: students, clinical educators, site managers, universities, clients

Planning for placements

Management of placements and learning programmes

Models of clinical education

Assessment of student performance

Giving and receiving feedback

Learning styles

Learning processes

Although we aim to provide an introductory workshop for our clinical educators in the field before they take their first student, this is not always possible, and in fact may not be necessary. Learning styles theory (see, for example, Honey and Mumford, 1986; Kolb, 1986) tells us that some learners in fact learn better by 'doing' first and then putting the theory around the experience. For these learners, participating in co-supervision of a student with a more experienced clinical educator colleague would be suitable. Linking novice clinical educators with experienced clinical educators or mentors is a desirable strategy regardless of the timing of initial preparation. We use this strategy frequently with new graduates, who can offer students some interesting caseload experiences and observation opportunities without having to take full responsibility for the planning, conduct and assessment of a placement. With novice clinical educators we are also careful about selecting students for placement with them. We try to send 'typical' or 'average' students whom we do not anticipate will cause the clinical educator undue stress or challenge. If early experiences of clinical education are pleasant and supported, novice clinical educators are more likely to continue to participate in clinical education.

Many resources such as readings, checklists, etc. will be provided at introductory workshops and in placement manuals, and other resources will be provided as indicated or on request. One of the most valuable resources a novice clinical educator can have is access to a university-based clinical placement support staff person. We suggest that such staff make regular times available to novice clinical educators throughout student placements, using phone, video-teleconference or face-to-face contact. Some of this contact can be one on one; some of it can be in groups with other clinical educators. What we aim to do in such groups is to establish a community of support and mentoring in clinical education.

Being part of a community of clinical educators is a good stimulus for developing or refining reflective practice as a clinical educator. Group members can encourage each other to journal and share aspects of their journals or critical incidents that arise from practice as a clinical educator. These groups can also provide much needed opportunities to debrief, dealing with negative as well as positive emotions associated with learning to be a clinical educator, perhaps using the Boud and Edwards' (1999) model of reflection outlined in Chapter 6. With the support offered by such groups and the learning that comes from both experience and consideration of theory of clinical education provided in workshops or readings, novice clinical educators can move on to the advanced beginner stage.

Professional development for the advanced beginner clinical educator

Professional development at this level is essentially about consolidation of previous knowledge and skill, and provision of opportunities to extend one's skills and capacity for reflection. We provide advanced beginners with more students who have different learning needs, and different levels of competence. We would not seek to give them particularly challenging students unless a more experienced clinical educator or university staff member was mentoring them. We would involve them in intermediate level workshops, which would emphasize learning from reflection and the development of personal and interpersonal skills. Refining teacher-as-manager skills would also be a topic for workshops and supportive discussions. We would encourage advanced beginners to be self-directed in developing their knowledge about clinical education through reading and networking. For some, participating in virtual communities of clinical educators using chat rooms is ideal. Table 8.7 summarizes the ideas presented in this section for facilitating development of advanced beginner level clinical educators.

Table 8.7 Learning strategies for advanced beginner clinical educators

More students with different learning needs, different levels of competence

Increased emphasis on reflection

Begin to network, use fora/chat rooms

Professional development for clinical educators at the competent stage

Competent clinical educators are those who have a good grasp of the theory and practice of clinical education. They are successful and efficient educators. What distinguishes them from clinical educators who seek professional artistry, according to the study by McAllister (2001), is that they do not actively seek challenges or take on new roles as clinical educators. Therefore professional development for competent clinical educators is about challenge and extension of skills and roles. Strategies for use with these clinical educators are listed in Table 8.8. We would challenge competent clinical educators by deliberately placing with them difficult students, or already excellent students who need extension. We would work in partnership with these clinical educators to develop, implement and evaluate teaching and learning strategies and opportunities with such students. We would also challenge competent clinical educators to try different models and approaches to clinical education perhaps piloting new structures for placements, e.g. when we were introducing system-wide multiple-student placements (i.e. two or more students with one clinical educator), we worked with already competent clinical educators to trial and report on this new placement structure. We also invite these competent clinical educators to become involved in cross-disciplinary supervision with colleagues and students from other health disciplines. Where possible, we encourage these competent clinicians to become involved in researching clinical education and evaluating innovative practice, and to co-author or co-present papers with university staff.

Table 8.8 Learning strategies for competent clinical educators

Challenge with difficult students, or students needing extension

Challenge to try different models/approaches, structures of placements

Involve in research, scholarship, evaluation of clinical education programmes

Involve in cross-disciplinary supervision

Become mentors of novice clinical educators

Strong personal and interpersonal skills and good self-knowledge make competent clinical educators ideal for mentoring novice and advanced beginner clinical educators. They can share their knowledge and expertise through co-supervision arrangements with novice colleagues at the same or a related work site, or adopt more formal mentoring roles using phone or video-conferencing or web contact with novices at a distance. Mentoring and support of a junior colleague also provide the impetus for enhancement of personal knowledge and skills, and may catalyse competent clinical educators to seek professional artistry.

Promoting professional artistry in clinical education

Professional artists seek to refine their personal and professional knowledge and skills further. A number of learning strategies can help clinical educators achieve these goals. These are listed in Table 8.9. Advanced level workshops, which give them opportunities to reflect on their practice, draw on the experiences of colleagues at similar levels of development, and derive new insights that can be supportive in refining and enhancing their practice as clinical educators. Heightening awareness of and responsiveness to gender, cultural and socioeconomic variables would be one goal of further professional development at this level. Professional artists in clinical education are well placed to take leadership roles in clinical education in their own and other health professions. They may provide leadership in multidisciplinary clinical education and supervision, and in professional supervision of peers in the workplace. They may sit on professional association committees developing policies or position papers pertinent to clinical education or on university boards or course reviews. They may become valued consultants to university programmes and clinical coordinators, assisting with the development and delivery of clinical education workshops for clinical educators at all levels of development. We would hope that they initiate research into clinical education and/or undertake higher degree studies in this area. We anticipate that they will be available for wise counsel and support to a range of colleagues concerned with clinical education. They can act as resources for clinical educators at all levels of development, particularly for those grappling with challenging students or ethical dilemmas. In addition we hope that this group of people are active advocates both within and beyond the profession for the critical importance of quality clinical education to the future of our profession and clients.

Table 8.9 Learning strategies for professional artists in clinical education

---

Heighten awareness of and responsiveness to gender, cultural and socioeconomic variables

Develop, prepare and run programmes for clinical educators

Provide leadership in multidisciplinary clinical education

Provide leadership in professional supervision of peers

Become resources/mentors for peers

Become consultants to university programmes and clinical coordinators

Hold formal university or professional association consultancy, committee roles or policy development

Initiate research into clinical education

Undertake higher degrees in clinical education

Advocate for the importance of quality clinical education to the future of our profession

---

Improving the status and recognition of clinical education and clinical educators

Clinical education is a low priority for many workplaces (Ferguson and Edwards, 1999). Sometimes this is because managers decide that it does not contribute positively to the workplace or the workflow. This view is held in the absence of any data to support it (Bristow and Hagler, 1997;

Ladyshewsky et al., 1994). In fact, research suggests that students may increase productivity of departments while on clinical placement (Short et al., 2001). There are also qualitative data from surveys, focus group interviews, etc. with clinicians and managers, which attest to the value of participation in terms of staff morale, professional development and staff recruitment (Meyers, 1995; Hancock and Hagler, 1998). However, sometimes participation in clinical education is held in low regard by clinicians themselves, who may feel that they do not have the time or want the responsibility of participation. Clinicians may also not see clinical education as a worthwhile career track activity because of its low status in many situations.

Clinical education needs to be accorded more status at all levels: within universities, in workplaces, within professional associations, within student bodies and within groups of clinical educators themselves. There needs to be recognition that the skills obtained by staff members through participation in clinical education are generalizable to roles that they may take with clients, in teams and in management, e.g. negotiation skills and conflict resolution skills practised and developed with students would be readily transferable to resolving issues as a team leader. Skills needed for the successful management of clinical placements could transfer to the skills needed to function as a department head. Furthermore, skills in clinical education and supervision of students lend themselves to workplace peer supervision and professional mentoring. There are many ways in which the status and recognition of clinical education could be raised. Table 8.10 lists some of these.

Table 8.10 Strategies for raising the status and recognition of clinical education

Appropriate funding for clinical education: placements, resources, staffing

Postgraduate speciality qualifications in clinical education

Partnerships between universities, workplaces and professional associations that emphasize mutual responsibility for clinical education

Creative placements that benefit both students and organizations

Recognition of excellence in the provision of clinical education by universities, students, workplaces, professional associations

Research into clinical education processes, costs/benefits of clinical education, outcomes in terms of client care and organizational service

Given the economic rationalist orientations to management prevailing in health services, targeted funding for clinical education is essential. In our experience, some workplaces argue that the provision of clinical education is a cost that they can no longer bear and ask universities to pay for placing students in their facilities, or to at least to contribute to the costs.

However, universities are often not funded to provide clinical education and are generally underfunded in all areas of activity. Government departments responsible for health and higher education need to resolve this problem, which is now critical in many countries. One model, which we have used successfully in Australia, is to work with health services to upgrade positions to that of 'student unit supervisor'. This is a senior level position and is responsible for the provision or organization and support of all clinical placements in a facility. Clinical educators in these positions are typically professional artists and have close links with the universities. Opportunities for increased funding and support for clinical education may be enhanced if evidence was available from research about the value of participation in clinical education for workplaces, and a true picture of the costs and benefits was available.

Another strategy that would raise the profile of clinical education and educators is the provision of specialty postgraduate qualifications in clinical education. This might be in the form of a university certificate, diploma, masters or doctoral level degree, using coursework, research or a combination of both. Such study could be undertaken face to face or by distance learning, or perhaps combine both at different stages of the programme. Students from a range of health disciplines in one or related sites could form real or virtual study groups, enhancing learning outcomes through bringing a range of professional perspectives to the group. Students undertaking such studies could engage with their lecturers in research into clinical education, which would serve further to highlight the importance of clinical education and refine its processes and outcomes.

Creative approaches to clinical education are also required. Although some professional associations are prescriptive about the nature of placements and levels of 'supervision' of students, our experience under more enlightened policies has been that students can undertake placements in non-traditional settings that make enormous contributions to their personal and professional development, as well as to the host site and its clients. These placements involve remote supervision by a speech–language pathology clinical educator, and/or supervision by on-site professionals of other disciplines.

The development of such innovative placements requires a collaborative rather than a directive interrelationship of professional associations, universities and workplaces. A sense of shared responsibility and mutual obligation for clinical education might flourish in such a relationship. There needs to be recognition that all three stakeholders have roles to play. Professional associations need to develop policies that support clinical education in contemporary workplace contexts and rewards for participation in clinical education, e.g. associations with mandatory or optional professional development/continuing education programmes could allow clinicians to claim participation in clinical education towards requirements. Professional associations might also create special honours and awards for clinical educators in the way that other forms of service to the profession are recognized. Universities also need to acknowledge and reward the efforts and contributions of sites and clinical educators, e.g. through formal awards for outstanding contribution, free continuing education or provision of research funds or support. Workplaces need to acknowledge the benefits that they receive from participation in terms of continuing education and professional development for staff, recruitment of new staff and retention of existing staff. They can also raise the profile of clinical education in their workplace by creating full-time senior level clinical educator positions.

Maintaining enthusiasm and interest in clinical education in the long term

Regardless of the status of clinical education, individual clinical educators still need to maintain their own interest and enthusiasm for the job over the long term, if the profession is not to lose competent clinical educators to burnout or stagnation. In Table 8.11 we offer some suggestions that we have used to help clinical educators maintain interest and enthusiasm for their role.

Some of these strategies are directed towards extending personal and professional knowledge and skills; some are about the avoidance of burnout. Others are directed towards creating diversity and novelty in the role of clinical educator, so that clinical educators can continue to develop towards professional artistry.

Conclusion

The continuum of professional development in clinical education, and goals and strategies discussed in this chapter, are congruent with the overall philosophy of this book. We have argued throughout this book that clinical education offers both students and clinical educators rich opportunities for professional development and that learning together can enhance such professional development. Students and clinical educators can form learning relationships based on humanistic values, which promote the development of a range of personal, interpersonal, cognitive and management skills, as well as knowledge needed for effective clinical practice. Assessment of self and others that empowers and promotes personal and professional development was considered. Strategies that promote the development of learning relationships, knowledge and skills are provided and illustrated throughout the book.

We believe that this book offers a unique perspective on clinical education, and challenges both clinical educators and students to seize the professional and personal development opportunities that entering into learning relationships in clinical education can offer.

Table 8.11 Ideas for maintaining enthusiasm and interest as a clinical educator

Improve your time management skills

Take time for self

Take breaks between placements

Have time out from clinical education from time to time

Find opportunities to do project work related to education

Maintain links with the university

Accept praise and thanks

Develop a personal learning plan so you can recognize your own growth

Keep your sense of humour

Undertake personal development work

Become involved in mentoring less experienced clinical educators

Get support from management for your role

Maintain appropriate boundaries between students and self, and home and work

Do not take undue responsibility for students who are failing

Do not always take the difficult students

Seek professional development even though you may already be competent

Become involved in policy development or research regarding clinical education

Provide professional development for other clinical educators, and thereby affirm your own professional artistry

References

Albert A, Munson R, Resnick M (eds) (1988) Reasoning in Medicine: An introduction to clinical inference. Baltimore, MD: John Hopkins University Press.

Alsop A, Ryan S (1996) Making the Most of Fieldwork Education: A practical approach. London: Chapman & Hall.

American Speech–Language–Hearing Association (1982a) Committee on Supervision in Speech–Language Pathology and Audiology. Minimum qualifications for supervisors and suggested competencies for effective clinical supervision. Asha 24: 339–342.

American Speech–Language–Hearing Association (1982b) Suggested competencies for effective supervision. Asha 24: 1021–1023.

American Speech–Language–Hearing Association (2001) Scope of Practice for Speech–Language Pathology and Audiology. Baltimore, MD: American Speech–Language–Hearing Association.

Anderson J (1988) The Supervisory Process in Speech–Language Pathology and Audiology. Boston, MA: College Hill.

Argyris C, Schön D (1974) Theory in Practice: Increasing professional effectiveness. San Francisco: Jossey-Bass.

Barrows HS, Feltovich PJ (1987) The clinical reasoning process. Medical Education 21: 86–91.

Baxter Magolda M (1992) Knowing and Reasoning in College: Gender related patterns in students' intellectual development. San Francisco: Jossey-Bass.

Belenky M, Clinchy B, Goldberger N, Tarule J (1986) Women's Ways of Knowing: The development of self, voice and mind. New York: Basic Books.

Benner P (1984) From Novice to Expert: Excellence and power in clinical nursing practice. Menlo Park, CA: Addison-Wesley.

Berne E (1966) Games People Play: The psychology of human relationships. London: Andre Deutsch.

Best D, Rose M (eds) (1996) Quality Supervision: Theory and practice for clinical supervisors. London: Saunders.

Biggs J, Telfer R (1987) The Process of Learning. Sydney: Prentice Hall.

Bortz M, Schoub B, McKenzie J (1992) Community work project in Gazankulu: A community based training experience. South African Journal of Communication Disorders 39: 62–67.

oshuizen H, Schmidt H (1992) On the role of biomedical knowledge in clinical reasoning by experts, intermediates and novices. Cognitive Science 16: 153–184.

Boshuizen H, Schmidt H (2000) The development of clinical reasoning expertise. In: Higgs J, Jones M (eds), Clinical Reasoning in the Health Professions, 2nd edn. Oxford: Butterworth-Heinemann, pp. 15–22.

Boud D (1989) The role of self-assessment in student grading. Assessment and Evaluation in Higher Education 14: 20–31.

Boud D (1992) The use of self-assessment schedules in negotiated learning. Studies in Higher Education 17: 185–200.

Boud D (2000) Sustainable assessment: Rethinking assessment for the learning society. Studies in Continuing Education 22: 151–167.

Boud D, Edwards H (1999) Learning for practice: Promoting learning in clinical and community settings. In: Higgs J, Edwards H (eds), Educating Beginning Practitioners: Challenges for health professional education. Oxford: Butterworth-Heinemann, pp. 173–179.

Boud D, Keogh R, Walker D (1985) Promoting reflection in learning: A model. In: Boud D, Keogh R, Walker D (eds), Reflection: Turning experience into learning. London: Kogan Page, pp. 18–40.

Brammer J (1996) The lived experience of clinical facilitation. Unpublished Master's thesis, University of New South Wales, Sydney.

Brasseur J (1989) The supervisory process: A continuum perspective. Language, Speech and Hearing Services in Schools 20: 274–295.

Bristow D, Hagler P (1997) Comparison of individual physical therapists' productivity to that of combined physical therapist–student pairs. Physiotherapy Canada winter: 16–23, 31.

Brookfield SD (1986) Understanding and Facilitating Adult Learning. Milton Keynes: Open University Press.

Callan C, O'Neill D, McAllister L (1994) Adventures in two to one supervision: Two students can be better than one. SUPERvision 18(1): 15–16.

Candy P, Crebert G, O'Leary J (1994) Developing Lifelong Learners through Undergraduate Education. Commissioned Report No. 28: National Board of Employment, Education and Training. Canberra, Australia: Australian Government Publishing Service.

Cant R, Higgs J (1999) Professional socialisation. In: Higgs J, Edwards H (eds), Educating Beginning Practitioners: Challenges for health professional education. Oxford: Butterworth-Heinemann, pp. 46–51.

Chan J, Carter S, McAllister L (1994) Contributors to anxiety in clinical education in undergraduate speech–language pathology students. Australian Journal of Human Communication Disorders 22(1): 57–73.

Cherniss C (1980) Staff Burnout Job Stress in the Human Services. Beverly Hills, CA: Sage.

Christie BA, Joyce PC, Moeller PL (1985) Fieldwork experience, Part II: The supervisor's dilemma. American Journal of Occupational Therapy 39: 675–681.

Clandinin DJ, Connelly FM (1991) Narrative and story in practice and research. In: Schön DA (ed.), The Reflective Turn: Case studies in and on educational practice. New York: Teachers College Press, pp. 258–281.

Clandinin DJ, Connelly FM (1994) Personal experience methods. In: Denzin N, Lincoln Y (eds), Handbook of Qualitative Research. Thousand Oaks, CA: Sage, pp. 413–427.

Connelly FM, Clandinin DJ (1988) Teachers as Curriculum Planners: Narratives of experience. New York: Teachers College Press.

Corey G, Corey M, Callanan P (1998) Issues and Ethics in the Helping Professions. Pacific Grove, OR: Brooks/Cole.

Crotty M (1996) Phenomenology and Nursing Research. Melbourne: Churchill Livingstone.

Crystal D (1997) English as a Global Language. New York: Cambridge University Press.

Csikszentmihalyi M (1990) Flow: The psychology of optimal experience. New York: Harper Row.

Culatta R, Seltzer H (1977) Content and sequence analysis of the supervisory session: A report of clinical use. Asha 19: 523–526.

Cupit R (1988) Student stress: An approach to coping at the interface between clinical and preclinical. Australian Journal of Physiotherapy 34: 215–219.

Cusick A (2001) Personal frames of reference in professional practice. In: Higgs J, Edwards H (eds), Practice Knowledge and Expertise in the Health Professions. Oxford: Butterworth-Heinemann, pp. 91–95.

Dodd B (1995) A problem solving approach to clinical management. In: Dodd B (ed.), Differential Diagnosis and Treatment of Children with Speech Disorder. London: Whurr, pp. 149–165.

Dowling S (2001) Supervision: Strategies for successful outcomes and productivity, 2nd edn. Boston, MA: Allyn Bacon.

Doyle J (2000) Teaching clinical reasoning to speech and hearing students. In: Higgs J, Jones M (eds), Clinical Reasoning in the Health Professions, 2nd edn. Oxford: Butterworth-Heinemann, pp. 230–235.

Drake V, Irurita V (1997) Clarifying ambiguity in problem fieldwork placements: Picking up and dealing with problem signals. Australian Occupational Therapy Journal 44: 62–70.

Dreyfus HL, Dreyfus SE (1986) Mind over Machine: The power of human intuition and expertise in the era of the computer. New York: Free Press.

Duchan J (2001) Impairment and social views of speech–language pathology: Clinical practices re-examined. Advances in Speech–Language Pathology 3: 37–45.

Edwards HM (1996) Clinical teaching: An exploration in three health professions. Unpublished PhD thesis, University of Melbourne, Melbourne.

Edwards I, Jones M, Carr J, Jensen G (1998) Clinical reasoning in three different fields of physiotherapy – A qualitative study. In: Proceedings of the Fifth International Congress. Melbourne: Australian Physiotherapy Association, pp. 298–300.

Egan G (1990) The Skilled Helper: A systematic approach to effective helping, 4th edn. Pacific Grove, OR: Brooks/Cole Publishing.

Elstein AS, Shulman LS, Sprafka SS (1978) Medical Problem Solving: An analysis of clinical reasoning. Cambridge, MA: Harvard University Press.

Emery MJ (1984) Effectiveness of the clinical instructor: Students' perspectives. Physical Therapy 64: 1079–1082.

Engel C (1995) Medical education in the 21st century: The need for a capability approach. Capability 1: 23–30.

Erickson E (1963) Childhood and Society, 2nd edn. New York: Norton.

Falchikov N, Boud D (1989) Student self-assessment in higher education: A meta-analysis. Review of Educational Research 59: 395–430.

Farmer S, Farmer J (1989) Supervision in Communication Disorders. Columbus, OH: Merrill Publishing.

Ferguson A, Elliot N (2001) Analysing aphasia treatment sessions. Clinical Linguistics Phonetics 15: 229–243.

Ferguson A, Fitzpatrick-Barr K (2001) Awareness of readiness for self-directed learning: A pilot study. In: Wilson L, Hewat S (eds), Evidence and Innovation: Proceedings of the 2001 Speech Pathology Australia national conference. Melbourne: Speech Pathology Australia.

Ferguson K, Edwards H (1999) Providing clinical education: The relationship between health and education. In: Higgs J, Edwards H (eds), Educating Beginning Practitioners: Challenges for health professional education. Oxford: Butterworth-Heinemann, pp. 52–58.

Fish D, Coles C (1998) Developing Professional Judgement in Health Care: Learning through the critical appreciation of practice. Oxford: Butterworth-Heinemann.

Fish D, Twinn S (1997) Quality Clinical Supervision in the Health Care Professions: Principled approaches to practice. Oxford: Butterworth-Heinemann.

Fleming M (1991) The therapist with the three track mind. American Journal of Occupational Therapy 45: 1007–1014.

Gilligan C (1993) In a Different Voice: Psychological theory and women's development, 2nd edn. Cambridge, MA: Harvard University Press.

Glaser R, Chi M (1988) Overview. In: Chi M, Glaser R, Farr M (eds), The Nature of Expertise. Hillsdale, NJ: Lawrence Erlbaum, pp. xvi–xxviii.

Glickman CD (1980) The developmental approach to supervision. Educational Leadership 38(Nov): 60–62.

Goffman E (1959) The Presentation of Self in Everyday Life. Garden City, NY: Doubleday, Anchor Books.

Goldhammer R, Anderson R, Krajewski R (1980) Clinical Supervision, 2nd edn. New York: Holt, Rinehart & Winston.

Goleman D (1995) Emotional Intelligence. New York: Bantam.

Gonczi A, Hagler P, Athanasou J (1993) The Development of Competency Based Assessment Strategies for the Professions. National Office of Overseas Skills Recognition, Research Paper No 8. Canberra: Australian Government Publishing Service.

Goodfellow J, McAllister L, Best D, Webb G, Fredericks D (2001) Students and educators learning within relationships. In: Higgs J, Titchen A (eds), Professional Practice in Health, Education and the Creative Arts. Oxford: Blackwell Science, pp. 161–174.

Hancock J, Hagler P (1998) A pilot study of the effects of SL-P practicum students on service delivery. Journal of Speech–Language Pathology and Audiology 22: 141–150.

Hargreaves A, Tucker E (1991) Teaching and guilt: Exploring the feelings of teaching. Teaching and Teacher Education 7: 491–505.

Hayes Fleming M, Mattingly C (2000) Action and narrative: Two dynamics of clinical reasoning. In: Higgs J, Jones M (eds), Clinical Reasoning in the Health Professions, 2nd edn. Oxford: Butterworth-Heinemann, pp. 54–61.

Heinrich K (1992) The intimate dialogue: Journal writing by students. Nurse Education 17: 1–21.

Henley E (1997) Operation India. Part Two. Australian Physiotherapy Association May: 22–27.

Henley E, Twible R (1997) Operation India – A unique fieldwork experience, Part One. Australian Physiotherapy Association NSW Bulletin March: 14–16.

Hewson MG, Jensen NM (1990) An inventory to improve clinical teaching in the general internal medicine clinic. Medical Education 24: 518–527.

Higgs J (1992) Managing clinical education: The educator manager and the self-directed learner. Physiotherapy 78: 822–828.

Higgs J (1993) The teacher in self-directed learning: Manager or co-manager. In: Graves N (ed.), Learner Managed Learning: Practice, theory and policy. London: World Education Fellowship, pp. 122–131.

Higgs J, Edwards H (eds) (1999) Educating Beginning Practitioners: Challenges for health professional education. Oxford: Elsevier LTD.

Higgs J, Hunt A (1999) Redefining the beginning practitioner. Focus on Health Professional Education: A Multidisciplinary Journal 1(1): 34–38.

Higgs J, Jones M (eds) (2000) Clinical Reasoning in the Health Professions, 2nd edn. Oxford: Butterworth-Heinemann.

Higgs J, Titchen A (2000) Knowledge and reasoning. In: Higgs J, Jones M (eds), Clinical Reasoning in the Health Professions, 2nd edn. Oxford: Butterworth-Heinemann, pp. 23–32.

Hofstede G (1997) Cultures and Organisations: Software of the mind, rev. edn. New York: McGraw-Hill.

Holly ML (1987) Keeping a Personal–Professional Journal. Geelong, Victoria: Deakin University Press.

Honey P, Mumford A (1986) The Manual of Learning Styles, 2nd edn. Berkshire: Authors.

Horton S, Byng S (2000) Examining interaction in language therapy. International Journal of Language Communication Disorders 35: 355–376.

Hunt A, Higgs J (1999) Learning generic skills. In: Higgs J, Edwards H (eds), Educating Beginning Practitioners: Challenges for health professional education. Oxford: Butterworth-Heinemann, pp. 166–172.

Irby DM (1986) Clinical teaching and the clinical teacher. Journal of Medical Education 61(9): 35–45.

Isaac K (2002) Speech Pathology in Cultural and Linguistic Diversity. London: Whurr.

Jager G (1994) Community based education in speech pathology and audiology at the University of Durban–Westville in an under served community. South African Journal of Communication Disorders 41: 93–102.

Jarski RW, Kulig K, Olson RE (1990) Clinical teaching in physical therapy: Student and teacher perceptions. Physical Therapy 70: 36–41.

Johnston S (1994) Conversations with student teachers – enhancing the dialogue of learning to teach. Teaching and Teacher Education 10(1): 71–82.

Jones M (1992) Clinical reasoning in manual therapy. Physical Therapy 72: 875–884.

Joshi S (1999) An investigation of supervisory style in speech pathology clinical education. Unpublished Masters thesis, University of Sydney, Sydney.

Joshi S, McAllister L (1998) An investigation of supervisory style in speech pathology clinical education. The Clinical Supervisor 17: 141–156.

Kadushin A (1968) Games people play in supervision. Social Work 18: 23–32.

Katz L (1972) Developmental stages of preschool teachers. Elementary School Education 73(1): 50–54.

Keating J (1993) Striving for a culturally appropriate speech pathology service in the Arctic. Australian Communication Quarterly Winter: 16–17.

Kenny B (1996) An investigation of self-evaluation by speech pathology students during supervisory conferences. Unpublished Masters thesis, University of Sydney, Sydney.

Kirschenbaum H, Henderson V (eds) (1990) The Carl Rogers Reader. London: Constable.

Knowles M (1980) The Modern Practice of Adult Education: From pedagogy to andragogy. New York: The Adult Education Co.

Kolb D (1986) Learning Styles Inventory: Technical manual. Boston, MA: McBer Co.

Krause H, Lee S-K, Covic T, Roberts R (2003) On the dimensional structure and psychological correlates of time management: Not much more than conscientiousness? Journal of Personality and Social Psychology in press.

Ladyshewsky R (1993) Clinical teaching and the 2:1 student to clinical instructor ratio. Journal of Physical Therapy Education 7: 31–35.

Ladyshewsky R (1995) Clinical Teaching. Canberra, Australia: HERDSA Gold Series.

Ladyshewsky R, Bird N, Finney J (1994) The impact on departmental productivity during physical therapy student placements: An investigation of outpatient physical therapy services. Physiotherapy Canada 46: 89–93.

Laycock M, Stephenson J (1994) Using Learning Contracts in Higher Education. London: Kogan Page.

Lincoln M, Adamson B, Covic T (2002) Learning time management skills: Why? When? Where and How? In: Williams C, Leitao S (eds), Journey from the Centre: Proceedings of the national conference of the Speech Pathology Association of Australia, Alice Springs, 20–23 May 2002. Melbourne, Victoria: Speech Pathology Association of Australia.

Lincoln M, Aron G (2001) Speech pathology students and voluntary work. ACQuiring Knowledge in Speech, Language and Hearing 3: 144–149.

Lincoln M, Carmody D, Maloney D (1997a) Professional development of students and clinical educators. In: McAllister L, Lincoln M, McLeod S, Maloney D (eds), Facilitating Learning in Clinical Settings. Cheltenham: Stanley Thornes, pp. 65–98.

Lincoln M, McAllister L (1993) Facilitating peer learning in clinical education. Medical Teacher 15: 17–25.

Lincoln M, McAllister L, Ferguson A, Harber R, Hagler P (2003) A national competency based assessment tool for speech pathology. Unpublished.

Lincoln M, McLeod S, McAllister L, Maloney D, Purcell D, Eadie P (1995) Learning styles of speech–language pathology students: A longitudinal investigation. Proceedings of the Conference of the Council of Supervisors in Speech–Language Pathology and Audiology – Clinical Supervision: Towards the 21st century, Cape Cod.

Lincoln M, Stockhausen L, Maloney D (1997b) Learning processes in clinical education. Professional development of students and clinical educators. In: McAllister L, Lincoln M, McLeod S, Maloney D (eds), Facilitating Learning in Clinical Settings. Cheltenham: Stanley Thornes, pp. 99–129.

Lubinski R (1994) Burnout. In: Lubinski R, Fratalli C (eds), Professional Issues in Speech–Language Pathology and Audiology: A textbook. San Diego, CA: Singular, pp. 345–358.

McAllister L (1997) An adult learning framework for clinical education. Professional development of students and clinical educators. In: McAllister L, Lincoln M, McLeod S, Maloney D (eds), Facilitating Learning in Clinical Settings. Cheltenham: Stanley Thornes, pp. 1–26.

McAllister L (2001) The experience of being a clinical educator. Unpublished PhD thesis, University of Sydney.

McAllister L (2002) Using adult learning theories: Facilitating others' learning in professional practice settings. In: Ryan S, Brown G, Esdaile L (eds), Becoming an Advanced Practitioner. Oxford: Butterworth-Heinemann.

McAllister L, Rose M (2000) Speech–language pathology students: Learning clinical reasoning. In: Higgs J, Jones M (eds), Clinical Reasoning in the Health Professions. Oxford: Butterworth-Heinemann, pp. 205–213.

McAllister L, Whiteford G (2002) Processes in the development of intercultural competence in speech pathology and occupational therapy students. Paper presented at the national conference of the Speech Pathology Association of Australia, Alice Springs, May. Melbourne: SPAA.

McCormack B (1992) Intuition: Concept analysis and application in curriculum development. 1. Concept analysis. Journal of Clinical Nursing 1: 339–344.

McInnis C, James R, Hartley R (2000) Trends in the first year experience in Australian universities. Evaluations and investigations programme. Canberra: Higher Education Division, DETYA.

McLeod S (1989) Responsibility, authority and power: A perspective on the role of the student supervisor. Australian Communication Quarterly 10: 10–12.

McLeod S, Romanini J, Cohn E, Higgs J (1997) Models and roles in clinical education. Professional development of students and clinical educators. In: McAllister L, Lincoln M, McLeod S, Maloney D (eds), Facilitating Learning in Clinical Settings. Cheltenham: Stanley Thornes, pp. 27–64.

Maloney D, Carmody D, Nemeth E (1997) Students experiencing problems learning in clinical settings. Professional development of students and clinical educators. In: McAllister L, Lincoln M, McLeod S, Maloney D (eds), Facilitating Learning in Clinical Settings. Cheltenham: Stanley Thornes, pp. 185–213.

Maloney D, Sheard C (1992) An interpersonal skills approach to the learning triad: Client, student and clinical educator. Paper presented at the annual conference of the Australian Association of Speech and Hearing, Melbourne, Australia.

Mandy S (1989) Facilitating student learning in clinical education. Australian Journal of Human Communication Disorders 17: 83–93.

Markus H, Nurius P (1986) Possible selves. American Psychologist Sept: 954–969.

Marton F, Saljo R (1984) Approaches to learning. In: Marton F, Hounsell D, Entwhistle N (eds), The Experience of Learning. Edinburgh: Scottish Academic Press.

Maslach C (1982) Burnout: The cost of caring. Englewood Cliffs, NJ: Prentice Hall.

Maslow A (1968) Toward a Psychology of Being, 2nd edn. Princeton, NJ: Van Nostrand.

Mattingly C, Hayes-Fleming M (eds) (1994) Clinical Reasoning: Forms of inquiry in therapeutic practice. Philadelphia: FA Davis.

Mawdsley B, Scudder R (1989) The integrative task–maturity model of supervision. Language, Speech, and Hearing Services in Schools 20: 274–295.

Meyers S (1995) Exploring the cost and benefit drivers of clinical education. American Journal of Occupational Therapy 49: 107–111.

Millwater J, Yarrow A (1992) Supervision of international practicums. In Yarrow A (ed.), Teaching Role of Supervision in the Practicum: Cross faculty perspectives. Brisbane, Australia: Queensland University of Technology, pp. 78–90.

Mullavey-O'Byrne C (1999) Issues in intercultural and international learning in health science curricula. In: Higgs J, Edwards H (eds), Educating Beginning Practitioners: Challenges for health professional education. Oxford: Butterworth-Heinemann, pp. 143–149.

Nemeth E (2004) The experience of being a student failing clinic: Their stories. Unpublished Master's honours research thesis, Charles Sturt University.

Neville S, French S (1991) Clinical education: Students' and clinical tutors' views. Physiotherapy 77: 351–354.

Nias J (1989) Primary Teachers Talking: A study of teaching as work. London: Routledge.

Noddings N (1984) A Feminine Approach to Ethics and Moral Education. Berkeley, CA: University of California Press.

Noddings N (1991) Stories in dialogue. In: Witherill C, Noddings N (eds), Stories Lives Tell: Narrative and dialogue in education. New York: Teachers College Press, pp. 157–171.

Onuoha A (1994) Effective clinical teaching behaviours from the perspective of students, supervisors and teachers. Physiotherapy 80: 208–214.

Padrick K, Tanner C, Putzier D, Westfall U (1987) Hypothesis evaluation: A component of diagnostic reasoning. In: McClane A (ed.), Classification of Nursing Diagnosis: Proceedings of the Seventh Conference. Toronto: Mosby, pp. 299–305.

Patel V, Groen G, Arocha J (1990) Medical expertise as a function of task difficulty. Memory and Cognition 18: 394–406.

Paukert J, Richards B (2000) How medical students and residents describe the roles and characteristics of their influential clinical teachers. Academic Medicine 75: 843–845.

Paul R (2002) Introduction to Clinical Methods in Communication Disorders. Baltimore, MA: Paul Brookes Publishing Co.

Perry W (1970) Forms of Intellectual and Ethical Development in the College Years. New York: Holt, Rinehart Winston.

Pickering M (1984) Interpersonal communication in speech–language pathology supervisory conferences: A qualitative study. Journal of Speech and Hearing Disorders 49: 189–195.

Pickering M (1987) Supervision: A person focussed process. In: Crago M, Pickering M (eds), Supervision in Human Communication Disorders: Perspectives on a process. Boston, MA: College-Hill, pp. 107–134.

Pickering M, McAllister L (1997) Clinical education and the future: An emerging mosaic of change, challenge and creativity. Professional development of students and clinical educators. In: McAllister L, Lincoln M, McLeod S, Maloney D (eds), Facilitating Learning in Clinical Settings. Cheltenham: Stanley Thornes, pp. 252–295.

Pickering M, McAllister L (2000) A conceptual framework for linking and guiding domestic cross-cultural and international practice in speech–language pathology. Advances in Speech Language Pathology 2: 93–106.

Polyani M (1958) Personal Knowledge. London: Routledge & Kegan Paul.

Price DA, Mitchell CA (1993) A model for clinical teaching and learning. Medical Education 27(1): 62–68.

Ray G (1984) Burnout: Potential problem for nursing faculty. Nursing and Health Care 5: 218–221.

Refshauge K, Higgs J (2000) Teaching clinical reasoning. In: Higgs J, Jones M (eds), Clinical Reasoning in the Health Professions, 2nd edn. Oxford: Butterworth-Heinemann, pp. 141–147.

Robertson S, Rosenthal J, Dawson V (1997) Using assessment to promote student learning. Professional development of students and clinical educators. In: McAllister L, Lincoln M, McLeod S, Maloney D (eds), Facilitating Learning in Clinical Settings. Cheltenham: Stanley Thornes, pp. 154–184.

Rogers C (1961) Becoming a Person. Boston, MA: Houghton Mifflin.

Rogers C (1962) The interpersonal relationship: The core of guidance. Harvard Educational Review 32: 116–129.

Rogers C (1967) Personal thoughts in teaching and learning. Merrill–Palmer Quarterly 3: 241–243.

Rogers C (1969) The characteristics of a helping relationship. In: Bennis W, Benne K, Chin R (eds), The Planning of Change. London: Holt, Rinehart & Winston, pp. 153–166.

Romanini J, Higgs J (1991) The teacher as manager in continuing and professional education. Studies in Continuing Education 13: 41–52.

Rose M, McAllister L, Best D (1999) Becoming a clinical educator. In: Higgs J, Edwards H (eds), Educating Beginning Practitioners: Challenges for health professional education. Oxford: Butterworth-Heinemann, pp. 271–277.

Rosenthal J (1986) Novice and experienced student clinical teams in undergraduate clinical practice. Australian Communication Quarterly 2: 12–15.

Sackett D et al. (2000) Evidence Based Medicine: How to practise and teach EBM, 2nd edn. Edinburgh: Churchill Livingstone.

Schmidt H, Norman G, Boshuizen H (1990) A cognitive perspective on medical expertise: Theory and implications. Academic Medicine 65: 611–621.

Schön DA (1983) The Reflective Practitioner. London: Temple-Smith.

Schön DA (1987) Educating the Reflective Practitioner. San Francisco: Jossey-Bass.

Seedhouse D, Lovett L (1992) Practical Medical Ethics. Chichester: Wiley.

Severiens S, Ten Dam G (1998) Gender and learning: Comparing two theories. Higher Education 35: 329–350.

Shanfield S, Hetherly V, Matthews K (2001) Excellent supervision: The residents' perspective. Journal of Psychotherapy Practice and Research 10(1): 23–27.

Short K, Gilsenan K, Lincoln M (2001) The evaluation of the impact of student placements on a large area Health Service. In: Wilson L, Hewat S (eds), Evidence and Innovation: Proceedings of the national conference of the Speech Pathology Association of Australia, Melbourne, 21–23 May 2001. Melbourne, Victoria: SPAA.

Sleight C (1984) Games people play in clinical supervision. Asha 26: 27–29.

Smith B (1987) Structured diaries. Training and Management Development Methods 1: 3.13–3.16.

Smith DL (2001) Facilitating the development of professional craft knowledge. In: Higgs J, Titchen A (eds), Practice Knowledge and Expertise in the Health Professions. Oxford: Butterworth-Heinemann, pp. 172–177.

Speech Pathology Association of Australia (2000) Code of Ethics, revised. Melbourne, Victoria: SPAA.

Speech Pathology Association of Australia (2001) The Competency-Based Occupational Standards for Speech Pathologists – entry level. Melbourne, Victoria: SPAA.

Speech Pathology Association of Australia (2002a) Labour Force Survey. Melbourne, Victoria: SPAA.

Speech Pathology Association of Australia (2002b) Ethics Education Package. Melbourne, Victoria: SPAA.

Speech Pathology Association of Australia (2002c) Scope of Practice for Speech Pathology. Melbourne: SPAA.

Staden H (1998) Alertness to the needs of others: A study of the emotional labour of caring. Journal of Advanced Nursing 27: 140–146.

Stengelhofen J (1993) Teaching Students in Clinical Settings. London: Chapman & Hall.

Stewart M, McAllister M, Rosenthal J, Chan J (1996) International Students in the Clinical Practicum. Problems with English language proficiency, cross-cultural communication and racism. Paper presented at the ISANA 7th annual conference, Waves of Change, Adelaide, August.

Stockhausen L, Creedy D (1994) Journal writing: Untapped potential for reflection and consolidation. In: Chen S, Cowdroy R, Kingsland A, Ostwald M (eds), Reflections on Problem Based Learning. Sydney, NSW: Australian Problem Based Learning Network, pp. 73–85.

Stritter FT, Hain JD, Grimes DA (1975) Clinical teaching re-examined. Journal of Medical Education 50: 876–882.

Swidler M, Ross E (1993) Burnout: A smouldering problem amongst South African speech–language pathologists and audiologists? South African Journal of Communication Disorders 40: 71–84.

Titchen A (1998) Professional craft knowledge in patient-centred nursing and the facilitation of its development. Unpublished PhD thesis, Oxford University.

Titchen A (2001) Critical companionship: A conceptual framework for developing expertise. In: Higgs J, Titchen A (eds), Practice Knowledge and Expertise in the Health Professions. Oxford: Butterworth-Heinemann, pp. 80–90.

Torbert WR (1978) Educating toward shared purpose, self-direction and quality work: The theory and practice of liberating structure. Journal of Higher Education 49: 109–135.

Trede F (2000) The role of knowledge and artistry in clinical expertise: A pilot study with rheumatology physiotherapists. Focus on Health Professional Education: A Multidisciplinary Journal 2: 1.

Weiler K (1988) Women Teaching for Change. New York: Bergin Garvey.

Williams P, Webb C (1994) Clinical supervision skills: A delphi and critical incident technique study. Medical Teacher 16: 139–155.

Yoder D, Kent R (1988) Decision Making in Speech–Language Pathology. Toronto: BC Decker.

Yoshikawa MJ (1987) The double-swing model of intercultural communication between the East and the West. In: Kincaid DL (ed.), Communication Theory. San Diego, CA: Academic Press, pp. 319–329.

Index